TWAYNE'S WORLD AUTHORS SERIES

A Survey of the World's Literature

Sylvia E. Bowman, Indiana University
GENERAL EDITOR

CHINA

William R. Schultz, University of Arizona
EDITOR

Chin Sheng-t'an

(TWAS 230)

TWAYNE'S WORLD AUTHORS SERIES (TWAS)

*The purpose of TWAS is to survey the major writers
—novelists, dramatists, historians, poets, philosophers,
and critics—of the nations of the world. Among the
national literatures covered are those of Australia,
Canada, China, Eastern Europe, France, Germany,
Greece, India, Italy, Japan, Latin America, the
Netherlands, New Zealand, Poland, Russia, Scan-
dinavia, Spain, and the African nations, as well as
Hebrew, Yiddish, and Latin Classical literatures. This
survey is complemented by Twayne's United States
Authors Series and English Authors Series.*

*The intent of each volume in these series is to present
a critical-analytical study of the works of the writer;
to include biographical and historical material that
may be necessary for understanding, appreciation,
and critical appraisal of the writer; and to present all
material in clear, concise English—but not to vitiate
the scholarly content of the work by doing so.*

Chin Sheng-t'an

By JOHN CHING-YU WANG

Stanford University

Twayne Publishers, Inc.   ::   New York

To My Wife

Acknowledgments

To The University of Chicago Press for material from James J. Y. Liu, *The Art of Chinese Poetry*, © 1962 by James J. Y. Liu; to Harvard University Press for material from William Hung, *Tu Fu: China's Greatest Poet*, Copyright 1952 by the President and Fellows of Harvard College; to Penguin Books Ltd. for material from A. C. Graham (tr.), *Poems of the Late T'ang*, Copyright © A. C. Graham, 1965.

Preface

Chin Sheng-t'an (1610?–1661) was one of the pioneers in China to advocate the importance of the traditionally despised vernacular literature. What makes him unique in the history of Chinese literature is that, unlike his predecessors who for the most part merely praised the vernacular works in general terms, he was able to demonstrate, through detailed critical commentaries, *how* these works excelled as works of literary art, and *how* they could be regarded as being on an equal footing with the standard classics. It was chiefly through his efforts that the vernacular literature began gradually to attain some popularity and prestige within the scholarly community, until shortly after the turn of the present century vernacular language works were finally admitted into the world of belles-lettres. Yet in spite of his importance in this development, I know of no serious effort either in China or elsewhere to examine his specific commentaries systematically and thoroughly, or to evaluate his critical procedure in general. The present study is an attempt to fill this rather conspicuous gap in the history of Chinese literary theory and criticism.

My primary interest here, then, is in Chin Sheng-t'an's literary criticism and in the role he played in the reevaluation of the literary worth of the traditional vernacular literature. His life story is told primarily as it relates to these aspects of his career. (We do not know much about him anyway.) Similarly, many of his miscellaneous writings, especially those highly specialized discourses on Buddhism and the *Yi-ching* (*Book of Changes*), are not discussed as they add little to our understanding of him as a literary critic. All this is of course but another way of saying that this is not meant to be an exhaustive study of Chin Sheng-t'an. Still, it is hoped that the reader, after having gone through the book, will at least have gained some understanding of what I consider to be Chin Sheng-t'an's most significant contributions in the world of letters.

CHIN SHENG-T'AN

In undertaking this study, I have had both the privilege and pleasure of receiving invaluable advice and help from many friends and teachers. I would especially like to express my sincere thanks to the following persons: Professors Harold Shadick and M. H. Abrams of Cornell University, Professor James I. Crump of the University of Michigan, Professor James J. Y. Liu of Stanford University, and Dr. Wang Ling of the Australian National University. Both the Center for Chinese Studies at the University of Michigan and the Center for East Asian Studies at Stanford have greatly facilitated the completion of this study by giving me successive summer research grants and other forms of financial help. The University of Chicago Press has kindly allowed me to quote from Professor James J. Y. Liu's *The Art of Chinese Poetry;* Penguin Books and Harvard University Press have done the same in connection with Dr. A. C. Graham's *Poems of the Late T'ang* (Penguin), Dr. William Hung's *Tu Fu: China's Greatest Poet,* and the late Dr. Richard G. Irwin's *The Evolution of a Chinese Novel.* To these various organizations I also would like to express my sincere thanks.

J.C.W.

Contents

Contents

Chronology

1610 (?)   Born in Soochow.

1625–   Obtained the *hsiu-ts'ai* degree.
1630 (?)

1641   Commentary on the *Shui-hu chuan* completed.

1644   Change of dynasty from Ming to Ch'ing.

1656   Wrote commentary on the *Hsi-hsiang chi* (according to the *Hsin-ch'ou chi-wen*). Sometime earlier he had started commenting on prose pieces selected from the *Tso-chuan* and other standard texts, which were eventually to be printed under the title, *Ts'ai-tzu pi-tu shu* (*Required Works for Geniuses*).

1660   Wrote a commentary on T'ang Regulated Verse of the seven-syllable type, known as the *T'ang ts'ai-tzu shih chia-chi* (*A First Collection of Poems by Geniuses of T'ang*).

1661   Decapitated for the alleged crime of "treason" while working on a commentary to Tu Fu's poetry.

CHAPTER 1

Chin and Some of His Predecessors

IN China, as late as the beginning of the present century, the word "literature" still meant almost exclusively the standard prose and poetry written in the *wen-yen* or literary language that had long since ceased to be used in everyday speech. Fiction and drama, written mainly in the living spoken language, were excluded from the realm of belles-lettres by the arbiters of taste. Although this disparagement of fiction and drama was not something unique to China,[1] that such a tendency should have persisted until so late a date is rather unusual. Two explanations may be ventured. First, according to Confucianism, the dominant school of thought in China for the past twenty centuries or so, the basic function of literature is to be found in cultivating moral character and polishing social behavior.[2] In both these respects, fiction and drama were not only considered to have a negligible positive moral value, but even to exert harmful influences.[3] Second, the traditional civil service examinations tested individuals in the Confucian classics and a few standard prose and poetry works —all written in the literary language. Since these examinations provided a sure, if not the only, way to fame and position, the study and mastery of the literary language became an urgent task for practically all scholars in old China. The literary language thus became a language of prestige. Scholars who had spent years acquiring a mastery of the classical language tended, quite naturally, to look down on any form of literature not written in it, and to view such writings as unorthodox and unfit for a man of culture.

With the abolition of the civil service examination system in 1905 and the fall of the old empire itself in 1911, the situation changed radically. By 1917 a group of young scholars under the inspiration and leadership of Hu Shih (1891–1962), a graduate of

Cornell then studying at Columbia University, started a Vernacular Literature Movement that finally won recognition for the vernacular language as a medium of written expression. Side by side
with the widespread adoption of the colloquial language came the
elevation of fiction and drama to the realm of pure, imaginative
literature ranking equally with, if not above, poetry and prose.

The Vernacular Literature Movement has been rightly regarded as a cultural event of major importance in the history of
modern China. But this event was not the result of a single stroke
of genius by Hu Shih and his followers. Neither did the so-called
Literary Revolution begin with the publication in 1917 of Hu
Shih's famous essay "Some Rough Suggestions for a Literary Reform" (Wen-hsüeh kai-liang ch'u-yi), nor even with the May
Fourth Movement of 1919, a national movement political, social,
and cultural in scope. More than two and half centuries earlier, a
group of nonconformist scholars (among them Chin Sheng-t'an)
had already initiated a cultural and intellectual trend which may
truly be termed a forerunner of the twentieth-century Vernacular
Literature Movement.[4] It started out as a reaction against en-
trenched literary values and practices of the time.

The literary world of early Ming times (the fourteenth and fifteenth centuries) had witnessed the rise of a powerful literary
movement known in history as the Antiquarian Movement (*fu-ku
yun-tung*).[5] As suggested by its name, it was a movement in
which the adherents asserted and actually tried to show that the
best way to learn how to write an essay or a poem is to go back to
the works of antiquity as models. However, they specified that not
all ancient works are fit to be used as models: only the essays of
the Ch'in (221–207 B.C.) and Han (206 B.C.–220 A.D.) dynasties
and the poems of the golden period of T'ang (*ca.* eighth century) were singled out by the Antiquarians to be worthy of imitation.[6] All the secrets and principles of essay and poetry writing, so
the Antiquarians argued, had been exhausted by writers of the
above-mentioned periods, and the best later writers could do was
to discover and apply the secrets and principles embodied in the
ancient models.

Inasmuch as literature, like any other human activity, is tradi-
tion-bound and cannot be said to be pure creation, the imitative
theory of the Antiquarians is justifiable and even plausible. In-

deed, this is exactly the basis on which Li Meng-yang (1472–1528), the founder and also the most prominent member of the Antiquarian Movement, tried to defend his theory of imitation: "Words must have methods and rules before they can fit and harmonize with musical laws, just as circles and squares must fit with compasses and rulers. The ancients used rules, which were not invented by them but really created by Nature. Now, when we imitate the ancients, we are not imitating the ancients but really imitating the natural laws of things." [7] By thus identifying imitation with the observance of the "natural laws of things," Li Meng-yang was able to render to the practice of imitation an air of dignity and respectability otherwise impossible.

However plausible and high-sounding his theory may be, in actual practice Li and his followers produced very little literature of enduring quality. Imitation of the "natural laws of things" became in reality wholesale stylistic borrowings from ancient writers. Numerous literary essays and poems were written, but at best they were merely echoes of the ancient models.

If the practice of the Antiquarians leaves much to be desired, their singling out of writers of particular periods for the purpose of imitation is even more unfortunate. Through such a procedure, many excellent writers of other periods were categorically rejected or ignored as inferior. Small wonder that in due course a strong reaction set in among men of independent spirit and mind, men who had the audacity to refuse to go along with the fashions of the day.

The first important dissenting voice came from Li Chih (1527–1602), philosopher, radical thinker, and scholar. Being strongly influenced by the teachings of the great philosopher Wang Yang-ming (1472–1529), Li Chih maintained that the most important thing in life is to preserve one's true self.[8] Paraphrasing Mencius, he characterized this true self as the "mind of the child" (*t'ung-hsin*), as being genuine, spontaneous, unbiased, and unobstructed by experience and ideas acquired through contacts with other people or through book learning. Li Chih was of course not objecting to social contacts and book learning as such. A sage, for example, could read books. The point is rather that "even if he does read a great deal, he will use [his reading] to protect this 'mind of the child' of his, so that it will not be lost." [9]

When applied to the field of literature, this theory of the "mind of the child" means specifically that any good piece of writing must be a genuine and spontaneous expression of the author's true self. Literature, in other words, must flow from the heart:

Since the mind of the child is obstructed . . . when the writer writes words and phrases, they will not be expressive enough. . . . It is because, the mind of the child being obstructed, the writer takes experience and ideas coming from outside as his true self. Since he takes experience and ideas [coming from outside] as his own true self, what he says is merely putting into speech this experience and these ideas; none of this comes from the mind of the child. Though the words may be carefully chosen, what do they offer us? Isn't it that as a false man the writer will speak false words, devote himself to false affairs, and write false essays? The person being false, whatever he does is nothing but falsehood. . . .[10]

The climax of the argument comes when he declares, "Never in the world has there been a superlative essay which has not come from the mind of the child." [11]

It follows naturally from such a view of literature that what counts most in writing is not how closely one can imitate a model or models, but rather how well one can express one's own feelings and wishes naturally and spontaneously. It is not surprising that Li Chih had little sympathy with the Antiquarians who, as we have seen, insisted that the only way to success in writing was through imitation. In another passage from the same essay we have just quoted, Li makes very clear why he disagrees with the whole Antiquarian Movement:

As for poetry, why should it be of the Ancient Verse type or of the types in the *Wen-hsüan* (*Ku Hsüan*)? [12] As for essays, why must they be from periods earlier than Ch'in? As we come down to the Six Dynasties, [the dominant form of literature] became poetry of the modern style (*chin-t'i*).[13] Later it became again the *ch'uan-ch'i* stories,[14] and again the *yuan-pen*[15] and the *tsa-chü*,[16] and again the *Hsi-hsiang chi* (*The Romance of the Western Chamber*), *Shui-hu chuan* (*Water Margin*), and the form that present scholars work at (*i.e.*, the eight-legged essay).[17] All of these are the most perfect writings of all times, and they cannot be judged on the principle of which was written first and which later.[18]

Two very important assertions are made in this short passage. First, that literature changes with time, that each period produces a particular type of literature of its own not to be ranked either higher or lower than other types of literature of other periods—a point, we might note, Hu Shih was later to pick up and use as a powerful argument for the recognition of vernacular literature.[19] Second, compelled by the logic of his "evolutionary theory of literature," if we may call it so,[20] Li does not hesitate to proclaim the high literary quality of such colloquial or semi-colloquial works as *The Romance of the Western Chamber* and *Water Margin*. Such an assertion, as noted by Liu Ta-chieh,[21] is perhaps the first such remark in the history of Chinese literature; it thus deserves special notice. As we shall see shortly, both points were later elaborated upon by other writers.

Although Li Chih spoke disparagingly of the Antiquarian Movement, he did so in a somewhat casual and offhand way. In fact, of the five literary works which he said he admired, the collection of Li Meng-yang's essays was one.[22] It was not until a few years later, when the three Yuan brothers (Yuan Tsung-tao, Yuan Hung-tao, and Yuan Chung-tao) became the dominant figures in the literary world of the latter part of the sixteenth century, that a counter-movement was consciously organized. Because the Yuans were natives of Kung-an, Hupeh, they and their followers are referred to as the Kung-an School. Of the three brothers, Yuan Hung-tao (1568–1610) was the most articulate and influential. He seems to have maintained a cordial relationship with Li Chih, whom he addressed as his teacher. In a touching short lyric entitled "Farewell to Teacher Lung-hu," he recorded his deep attachment for Li:

> After ten days of sojourn, the time to part arrives unawares;
> There is no plan to return again.
> Stepping out the door, with tear-filled eyes,
> In the end, I fail to be a man of strong heart.[23]

Elaborating on Li Chih's idea that literature changes with time, Hung-tao writes in a preface to a collection of writings by one of his friends: "The reason why literature cannot but evolve from what is ancient to what is modern is because of the dictates of

time. . . . The ancients had their own time, while the moderns
also have their own time. For a modern writer to copy the words
of the ancients and pretend that what he has written is the style of
antiquity would be like wearing summer hemp clothes in bitter
winter." [24] And he goes on to explain in greater detail than Li Chih
how each literary form, after having reached its zenith, naturally
gives way to another new form, and how worn-out literary practices of certain periods are superseded by more appropriate
conventions. He does not object to looking back to writers of antiquity for general guidance and inspiration. But when this degen-
erates into what amounts to slavish copying, he has little sympathy
or patience. He continues:

It was not until recent times that the literati began to outdo each
other in promoting the theory of returning to antiquity. If it were just
a matter of going back to antiquity, there would be nothing wrong.
But what the literati have actually done is to steal from and plagiarize
the ancient writers, and to call this going back to antiquity. They
model every sentence and every word [upon old examples] and endeavor to be associated [with the ancients]. Ignoring what is actually
in front of them, they collect worn-out words and sentences. The
talented, restricted by models, dare not develop their own talents. The
mediocre merely select a few empty sentences and patch them together
to form a poem. The intelligent ones are restricted by tradition, while
the stupid are contented with the ease of copying. When one man
shouts [the slogan of imitation], millions echo him. Alas, it is really
shameful that poetry has deteriorated to such a state. [25]

Hung-tao's effort to discredit the Antiquarian Movement was
supported by similar arguments from his two brothers. Reinforc-
ing the "evolutionary theory of literature," Hung-tao's younger
brother Chung-tao said, "No literary form lasts a century without
change." [26] Like his brother Hung-tao, he does not object to the
idea of imitating the ancient writers; but what he cannot tolerate
is the mere imitation of outer appearance while completely ignoring the true spirit of the ancient writers. Tsung-tao, Hung-tao's
older brother, argues against the Antiquarians from still another
angle: since language, the medium of literature, is constantly in a
process of change, it would be foolish for modern writers to imitate a language that has ceased to be used for a long time. Fur-

thermore, the difficult, obscure ancient language we are told to imitate may have very well been the language of the common people of former times. In his own words:

Speech is something that represents thought, and writing is something used to stand for what is said. Being twice removed from the source, even though writing may be lucid and fluent, it is, we fear, already not as good as speech; how much less can it approximate to what is in the mind? That is why Confucius in discussing composition said, "The purpose of writing is to communicate, and that is all." Whether a piece of writing is literature or not can be judged by whether it communicates or not. Of the writings of T'ang, Yü, and the Three Dynasties (*i.e.* Hsia, Shang, and Chou), there are none which are not expressive. Nowadays, when people, in reading ancient texts, cannot immediately understand their meaning, they will say that ancient writings are exotic and obscure (*ch'i ao*), and that therefore writers of today should not write in a simple and easy-to-understand (*p'ing yi*) style. However, in time there is the distinction of ancient and modern, in language there is also the distinction of ancient and modern. How do we know that what are called exotic words and obscure sentences by present-day writers were not the common speech found in the streets and alleys in ancient times? [27]

What is important in writing, according to the Yuan brothers, is to express what Hung-tao calls one's "true nature" (*hsing-ling*) in a natural and spontaneous way. Like many other traditional scholars in China, Hung-tao did not bother to define clearly what he meant by one's "true nature." But from his writings in general, we may assume that he used the term to mean a quality with which a person is born, and which is not to be acquired through social contacts or learning. It is in fact but another term for Li Chih's "mind of the child." Thus Hung-tao writes in a preface to an anthology of his younger brother Chung-tao's poems:

The majority of Hsiao-hsiu's (*i.e.* Chung-tao's) poems simply express his "true nature," and are not restricted by a definite form or model (*ko-t'ao*). If the words did not flow out from his breast, he would not lift his pen. Sometimes, his feeling being blended perfectly with the outside world, he would produce thousands of words in an instant, as [naturally and fluently as] water flows eastwards [toward the ocean]. . . . In his diction, there are good expressions as well as bad ones.

There is no need to comment on the good ones. But even the bad ones abound in terms that are original (*pen-se*) and unique (*tu-tsao*).[28]

Like Li Chih who, compelled by the logic of his literary theory, acknowledged the merits of the *Shui-hu chuan* and *Hsi-hsiang chi*, the Yuan brothers also praised popular literature in the most glowing terms. In the preface to his brother's poems we have quoted above, Hung-tao remarks emphatically:

Therefore, I say that the poetry and prose of today will not be passed on to later generations. The pieces that have one chance in ten thousand of being passed on to later generations are probably folks songs, such as the *Po p'o yü* (*Break the Jade*) or the *Ta-ts'ao kan* (*Grass Beating Stick*), songs sung by women and children in the back alleys. Being compositions by ignorant but unaffected people (*chen-jen*), they are invested with a genuine tone (*chen-sheng*). [These unaffected people] do not try to imitate [the authors] of the Han and Wei Dynasties or walk in the footsteps of those in the golden period of T'ang. They express themselves freely without inhibition and thus are able to communicate the happiness and sorrow, the anger and joy, the appetites and preferences, the feelings and desires of a human being. This is a heartening situation.[29]

Of the popular works, Hung-tao particularly admired the *Shui-hu chuan*, which he ranks even above the Six Classics and Szu-ma Ch'ien's *Shih-chi* (*Records of the Grand Historian*). A poem entitled "Upon Hearing the Story of *Shui-hu chuan* Recited by Mr. Chu" (*T'ing Chu Sheng shuo Shui-hu chuan*) contains the following lines (the first six lines):

> When young I was good at humorous stories,
> I reveled in the lives of the jesters.[30]
> Later when I read the *Shui-hu* story,
> Its writing was still more fascinating and unusual.
> The Six Classics are no longer the model of style;
> Even Ssu-ma Ch'ien fails in elegance.[31]

Yet for all their praise of vernacular literature, neither Li Chih nor the Yuan brothers actually tried to demonstrate or actually succeeded in demonstrating how the vernacular literature could achieve literary excellence,[32] and thus be placed on a par with classical literature. The task was left for Chin Sheng-t'an to com-

plete less than half a century later, an investigation of which will
constitute the main part of this study.

Like his predecessors, Li Chih and the Yuan brothers, Chin believed that literature ought to be the expression of what one genuinely feels at heart, and that it should not be bound in the shackles
of ancient models. Thus he said: "It has always been that a literary composition derives from one's own 'true nature' (*hsing-ling*),
and is then allowed to swing and sway at its own will. As soon as
it is weighed down by [the precedents of] previous writers, it will
never be able to set itself free from the trap again." [33] Similarly, he
maintained that genius is something that cannot be confined to
any one particular literary period or any one particular author. He
said matter-of-factly, "Chuang Chou (*i.e.* Chuang-tzu) possesses
the genius of Chuang Chou; Ch'ü P'ing (*i.e.* Ch'ü Yuan) possesses
the genius of Ch'ü P'ing; Ma Ch'ien (*i.e.* Szu-ma Ch'ien) possesses the genius of Ma Ch'ien; Tu Fu possesses the genius of Tu
Fu; and on down until we come to Shih Nai-an who possesses the
genius of Shih Nai-an, and Tung Chieh-yuan who possesses the
genius of Tung Chieh-yuan." [34] For this reason, Chin did not hesitate to rank the *Shui-hu chuan* and *Hsi-hsiang chi* on an equal
footing with such classical works as the *Chuang-tzu, Li Sao* (*On
Encountering Sorrow*), *Shih-chi*, and the poetry of Tu Fu, and
called these works collectively the *Six Works of Genius* (*Liu ts'ai-
tzu shu*).

Unlike his predecessors, however, Chin was not satisfied to
praise these vernacular works in general terms. No sooner had he
designated them as works of genius, than he proceeded to prove
his point by providing a commentary for each one of them in a
thorough and detailed manner unprecedented in the history of
Chinese literary criticism. Commenting on Chin's edition of the
Hsi-hsiang chi, Li Yü (1611–1680), a younger contemporary of
Chin, who was himself a playwright and esteemed drama critic,
said, "From the appearance of the *Hsi-hsiang chi* until now, more
than four hundred years have elapsed. Those who have considered it to be the number one play in excellence number I don't
know how many tens and thousands. But as for demonstrating in
detail why it is so, there is only one Chin Sheng-t'an. . . . There
is not a single sentence, or a single word in the play, the reason
and intention of whose existence he will not trace or seek out." [35]
What Li Yü has said about the *Hsi-hsiang chi* applies just as well

to the *Shui-hu chuan.* It is here, I feel, that Chin made his most valuable contribution in this first attempt in China to elevate fiction and drama to their proper place, and it is also here that he left a permanent mark in the general history of Chinese literary criticism.

Besides the *Shui-hu* and *Hsi-hsiang* commentaries, Chin's other noteworthy critical effort was his commentary on about 180 poems in various forms by Tu Fu. Though historically less significant, it yet sheds illuminating light on Chin's characteristics as a commentator, and is indispensable in understanding his literary criticism as a whole. In the following chapters we shall examine in detail these various commentaries. Before we do, however, we need to know something about the man and his literary views in general.

CHAPTER 2

His Life

IN spite of Chin's great fame and popularity as a commentator, we know surprisingly little about the details of his life. His tragic death for the alleged crime of "treason" may have deprived him of the privilege of an entry in the local chronicles and other standard histories. As a result, the best first-hand accounts we now have of Chin's life—besides scattered references in his own writings—are a brief biography of about 700 words by Liao Yen (1644–1705), a younger contemporary and ardent admirer of his,[1] and two chronicles by anonymous authors about the circumstances of his death—*K'u-miao chi-lüeh* (*A Brief Record of the Incident of Lamenting in the Temple*) and *Hsin-ch'ou chi-wen* (*A Chronicle of the Year Hsin-ch'ou, i.e. 1661*).[2] To make things worse, the little we do know about him is so imbedded in legends of all kinds that we have to be constantly on guard not to mix fact with hearsay.[3]

The paucity of reliable information about Chin is reflected in the fact that there are only two moderately extensive biographical treatments of him by modern scholars—Karashima Takeshi's "Kin Sei-tan no shōgai to sono bungei hihyo" ("The Life and Literary Criticism of Chin Sheng-t'an") and Ch'en Teng-yuan's *Chin Sheng-t'an chuan* (*A Biography of Chin Sheng-t'an*).[4] In neither case is the image of Chin as a man brought out clearly, and one cannot help feeling that both biographers have spun out their material too thin. The best accounts of Chin's life and thought remain Fang Chao-ying's short essay in Hummel's *Eminent Chinese of the Ch'ing Period* [5] and Richard Irwin's slightly longer section in his *The Evolution of a Chinese Novel*.[6] In what I have to say of Chin's life I cannot claim to have discovered new facts. But having been able to compare all the preceding studies and having gone through Chin's various critical commentaries at some length,

23

I hope my account will add something to our understanding of his character and thought. His life readily falls into two main periods.

I   His Life under the Ming (1610?–1644)

Chin's personal name was Jen-jui. Sheng-t'an, the name by which he is more often referred to, was his *tzu*.[7] When he was born we do not know. Basing their computation on the fact that in 1641 his son Yung was nine years old (10 *sui*), both Karashima Takeshi and Ch'en Teng-yuan place his birth around 1610,[8] and this date has been accepted by other scholars.[9]

We know little about Chin's family except that they came from Wu Hsien (better known as Soochow), and, most likely, he lived there all his life. The family belonged to the scholar-gentry class. His father was evidently a scholar of some sort, for Chin recalls in his Third Preface to the *Shui-hu chuan,* "I noticed that my father would often chant from these books (*i.e. The Four Books*) throughout the night, [as though] he were very happy." [10] Chin himself was well versed in all the Confucian classics, and he subsequently earned the *hsiu-ts'ai* degree.[11]

The family, however, was not prosperous: Chin was sent to a village school instead of being tutored privately at home.[12] Moreover, the family seems to have been plagued by sickness and death. Years later when he came to a passage in the *Shui-hu chuan,* where a character merely pretends to be seriously ill, he was deeply moved and wrote in his comments: "Even when I was young, a great many members of my family died or were dangerously ill, and when I suddenly came upon this passage, my tears rolled down involuntarily." [13] Family finances did not improve as he grew up. In his Explanatory Notes to the *Hsi-hsiang chi,* he tells of plans to print a collection of more than a hundred model essays annotated by himself for the instruction of his son and nephews. "But unfortunately," he writes, "because of deaths in the house and turmoil in the country my family is poor and without capital. Therefore to this day my wish remains unfulfilled." [14] His cousin Chin Ch'ang reported to the same effect: "In his Ch'ang-ching (Intoning the Classics) Study were all the books he had read and they were truly works most men have never even seen . . . Once I asked him privately, 'Why not have them printed and circulated?' He answered reluctantly, 'I am poor and have no money.' " [15]

Chin started his formal schooling rather late at the age of nine. Immediately, he tells us, he began to demonstrate his independence of spirit by questioning the worth of the study of the Confucian classics:

> It was not until I was nine years old (10 *sui*) that I attended the local school. As was the custom, we studied the *Great Learning*, the *Doctrine of the Mean*, the *Analects*, and the *Mencius* (*i.e. The Four Books*). But I was very bored. Often I would whisper to the other boys, "What is the purpose of studying these books?" Furthermore, I noticed that my father would often chant from these books throughout the night [as though] he were very happy. I could never understand why. I used to wonder how many books there were altogether in the world. What did they all say? Wouldn't there be any repetitions? Questions such as these I could never get clear in my mind.[16]

His intellectual curiosity was not always treated kindly by his teacher. Once, when reading the *Analects*, he came upon the following passage: "Tzu-chang asked, 'What must a scholar do so that he may be considered a success?' Confucius replied, 'What kind of success do you mean?' " [17] Apparently surprised by the somewhat abrupt and harsh tone implied in the Master's response, Chin stuck out his tongue involuntarily. For this rude action, he was scolded and given a good flogging.[18] But for all his unruliness and unusual ideas, Chin proved to be a good and conscientious student. In his Introductory Remarks to Chapter 56 of the *Shui-hu chuan*, he writes: "When I was quite young, I used to sit by the window in the local school and read. When it was getting dark, I would stop reading; the sun would have gone down, and no more light came through the window. Several years passed in this way as if they were a single day. Even now, whenever the window darkens in the evening twilight, I feel as though I were still in my old school." [19]

If he was diligent enough studying the standard classics assigned in school, he was much more affected by the works of pure literature he encountered out of school. He tells us that one day, reading the *Hsi-hsiang chi*, he came upon these words in Part I, Act III: "If she won't even look at me, what am I to do?" [20]

He silently put away the book and went to bed for three or four days without speech, food, and drink—completely overwhelmed by the special force these words happened to communicate to him. His opportunity to enjoy books other than the classics came at ten when he was several times forced to stay out of school on account of a minor illness.[21] Unlike most children of that age who enjoy playing, his great delight was poring over books unsupervised by a school teacher. Among the many works he discovered that year were the *Lotus Sutra* (*Saddharmapundarika*), Ch'ü Yuan's *Li Sao*, Szu-ma Ch'ien's *Shih-chi*, and the current edition of the *Shui-hu chuan*. Although he liked all of these works—an unusual thing for a child of ten, the one he loved most was the *Shui-hu chuan* which he "clasped to his bosom day and night." Next year, at the age of eleven, he found an old edition of the *Shui-hu chuan* in the Kuan-hua Study of his friend Han Chu, who apparently also came from Soochow. Overjoyed with the discovery, he labored day and night to make a copy of his own, and even accompanied it with his youthful comments. This undertaking took him almost five months. His early enthusiasm for these books eventually led him in his adult years to pronounce them (except for the *Lotus Sutra*) great works of literature written by men of genius.

At a time when most scholars occupied themselves almost exclusively with the mastery of the Confucian classics for the civil service examinations, Chin's demonstration of such enthusiasm for popular literature and Buddhist and Taoist writings at such a tender age is a good measure of his intellectual independence and the particular personality he was to develop as he matured. Chin seems to have been aware of this. "When I was a child," he recalls in his commentary on Tu Fu's poems, "I thought myself to be possessed of enormous talents."[22] This awareness did not make him feel particularly happy, as he continues, "I felt terribly disappointed, as though from ancient times until now I alone had great talents, but I alone remained frustrated and unknown."[23]

The commonest way to achieve fame was by taking the civil service examinations. Like most scholars of his time Chin tried it (probably in his late teens), and succeeded in obtaining the *hsiu-ts'ai* degree, the lowest of the three degrees in the examination system.[24] He is said to have compiled a collection of the so-called eight-legged essays,[25] the type required in the examination. This would indicate that he probably planned to sit for a higher degree. But there is no record that he ever obtained a more advanced degree.

Perhaps he decided not to seek an advanced degree, for he was an individualist bent on pursuing his own likes and dislikes, and the exacting, restrictive civil service examination system may have proven unpalatable. An intimate glimpse of his individualist traits, or at least of his delight in the unconventional, is provided in the so-called "Thirty-three Delights in Life," which he and his good friend Wang Cho-shan counted one day when they were staying at an inn.[26] Here we see vividly his enjoyment of things purely sensory, his love of personal freedom, and a certain tendency toward mischievousness. The cutting of a watermelon on a summer day and the bathing of scabby sores behind closed doors, for example, both afforded him immeasurable pleasure. To him, the joy of being a magistrate would be to beat the drum to dismiss the court. One way to amuse himself on a spring night when half-intoxicated was to shoot off a dozen or so large firecrackers. He declared he would have become a monk only were he allowed to eat meat in public, and then he would shave his head only on a hot summer day! And so on. But let Chin speak for himself:

On a spring night, drinking heartily with several high-spirited friends, I become half drunk. It is hard to stop; it is also hard to go on. An understanding boy at the side suddenly brings in some big firecrackers, ten or so in all. I then get up, go outside, and fetching a lighter, set them off. The fragrant smell of sulphur enters my brain through the nostrils, and I feel exhilarated all over. Is this not delightful?

On a summer day, I take out a sharp knife and cut a dark green watermelon on a vermilion plate. Is this not delightful?

I have wanted to become a monk for a long time. The trouble is monks are not allowed to eat meat in public. If I could be a monk and still eat meat publicly, I would with the help of hot water and a sharp razor shave my head clean some summer month. Would this not be delightful?

To have three or four scabby sores in a private part of one's body and to be able now and then to ask for hot water to scald them behind closed doors. Is this not delightful?

To be a magistrate and everyday order the drum beaten to retire, is this not delightful?

These accounts should not be taken too literally. They may or may not correspond to actual events in Chin's life. Furthermore, Chin says, the "Thirty-three Delights" were recalled some twenty years after the occasion, and he could no longer remember which of them actually belonged to his friend Cho-shan, and which were his own. Yet, when viewed as a whole (and remembering Chin and his friend evidently had many things in common),[27] these passages may serve as a fair indication of the kind of tastes Chin cultivated during this period.

His individualism as revealed in the "Thirty-three Delights in Life" can also be seen in reports about him by friends and close associates. Writing in a preface to Chin's posthumously printed commentary on a group of prose works known as the *Ts'ai-tzu pi-tu shu* (*Required Works for Geniuses*), Hsü Tseng thus says, "Sheng-t'an was by nature free and unconventional (*shu-tang*), and fond of leisure and relaxation. His favorite spots were along the water edges and in the woods. He was also fond of drinking. Everyday he was invited by his drinking friends. If not, he would become listless. Sometimes when his spirits were high, he would write commentaries for books. Brandishing his brush like wind, he could finish one or two *chüan* in a day. In less than three days, however, his spirits would reach a low ebb, and his drinking friends would again drag him away." [28]

The last years of Ming, as can be expected of a declining dynasty, were a dark period both socially and politically. Inside the court, eunuchs plotted intrigues against the more capable ministers. Outside, people suffered under oppressive local officials and powerful gentry. Added to this gloomy situation was widespread banditry causing havoc throughout the country. Late Ming society, as reflected in the *Chin p'ing mei*, seems shrouded in a kind of *fin de siècle* spirit marked by corruption, moral turbidity, and utter chaos.

Under such circumstances, perhaps as a way to channel personal feelings of frustration, Chin began to assume a pose purposely meant to be arrogant and offensive. "When sorrow and depression come upon you," he says in his comments on one of Tu Fu's poems, "how can you dispel them? One way to comfort yourself is probably by speaking loudly of your own importance while turning the whites of your eyes upon other people." [29] And this is exactly what he seems to have done. According to his biographer

Liao Yen, to ridicule scholars renowned as public lecturers Chin would sometimes demonstrate his vast acquaintance with books both orthodox and unorthodox by holding public forum himself, to the infinite delight and admiration of large crowds, but to the great discomfiture of other scholars:

Often there were those who became known for expounding on philosophical texts (*chiang hsüeh*). He would immediately rise up to refute them. He set up a platform in the Kuan-hua Study where he was residing, summoned students, and gave a lecture he called "The Samadhi of the Enlightenment of a Sage" (Sheng tzu-chüeh san-mei). He carried and looked over his own manuscripts, and [kept them so] secret [that he would] not show them to anyone. Whenever he mounted the platform and started to talk, his voice was loud and clear, and he would look around majestically. Nothing—be it classics, history, philosophy, literary works, book commentaries, or the various inner and outer Buddhist sutras and Taoist scriptures, or novels and all kinds of fictitious histories—escaped mention. He expounded these various works backward and forward, connecting them with a single principle, until no meaning was left unexplained. The audience below the platform, among whom were Buddhist monks, would prostrate themselves in obeisance, and sigh that [this was something] they had never heard before. He would then clap his hands and look self-important. Even though the other lecturers hearing his talks knitted their eyebrows and moaned [to show disapproval], he paid no attention.[30]

But we should not conclude from this account by Liao Yen that Chin spent all his time doing nothing more constructive than ridiculing public lecturers, for it was during this period that he began writing the commentary to the *Shui-hu chuan*. We have no information about when he started this work. Although he himself claimed, as we have seen above, that he had already written comments to the book at the age of eleven, it is doubtful if any of those juvenile observations were incorporated in the commentary as it exists today. Whatever the case, since the Third Preface to his commentary is dated the fifteenth day of the second month of 1641, we may say with assurance that the commentary was completed within the period with which we are now concerned.

The *Shui-hu* commentary, to be examined in detail in Chapter 4, sheds some interesting light upon the character of Chin. The most striking aspect of the commentary is its revelation of his per-

sonal vanity. He was extremely conscious of his own critical
power and insight. So much was this the case that he did things
which are quite indefensible in a critic. For example, he frequently changed the text of the original without textual or historical basis and then hailed his own emendations as "extraordinary"
(*ch'i*) or "marvelous" (*miao*). Often not satisfied with this kind of
self-flattery, he sometimes stated quite bluntly just how good his
comments were. In his Introductory Remarks to Chapter 12, after
having pointed out the hidden excellence of the writing in the
chapter, he declared boldly, "Since the invention of pen and ink,
there has never been finer writing. Since the existence of such
writing, there have never been finer commentary." [31] In all fairness
to Chin, what he says about his own emendations and comments
must be acknowledged to be largely true. But to have gone so far
out of his way to impress this on others is exactly what some readers find so hard to accept in him.

The commentary also reveals a contentious disposition. When
he had a viewpoint to advance, he would do everything possible
to advance it. The novel in its original form is basically a glorification of the exploits of a group of bandits who advocated a kind of
rude justice. For fear such a theme would encourage the already
widespread banditry of his time, Chin, although he showed sympathy toward the bandits as individuals, condemned them as a
group.[32] In order to win the reader over to his side of the argument, he did a number of things. First, he offered an ingenious
but impossibly fanciful interpretation of the title of the novel,
which in reality means simply "The Story [of the Bandit Lair] in
the Marsh." "As for the expression 'Water Margin' used by Shih
Nai-an (*i.e.* the author), [it implies that] at the edge of the king's
land, there is 'water' and outside the water there is the 'margin'
(*i.e.* the bank). [This means that Nai-an wished to] place them
far away. The reason for placing them far off is that they are the
malignant things in the world, [and malignant things are what]
all the people of the world condemn; they are the evil things of
the world, [and evil things are what] all the people in the world
despise." [33] Next he proceeds to single out Sung Chiang, the leader
of the group, for a number of unfounded and vicious attacks.[34]
Still not certain that he has made his point, he again demonstrates
his unscrupulousness as a critic by simply cutting out the final fifty
chapters of the novel in which the bandits are pardoned and en-

listed in the service of the imperial army—and substituting his own final chapter in which the bandits are all put to death in a dream by one of the leaders.[35] On top of this he claims that his edition was based on an "old text" by Shih Nai-an,[36] and the discarded portion was simply the petty work of Lo Kuan-chung.[37] Then, to reinforce his claim, he forges a preface to his edition of the novel and appends to it the name of Shih Nai-an of Tung-tu! [38]

But perhaps the most significant aspect of Chin's character as revealed by the commentary is his basic—and very Chinese—ambivalence: he is inclined to live a laissez-faire life in the Buddhist-Taoist sense of the word on the one hand, but feels the urge to participate in worldly affairs (a distinctly Confucian trait) on the other.

This Buddhist-Taoist inclination, doubtless intensified by the political and military upheavals of his time, makes him keenly aware of the transitory nature of life. When in Chapter 14 he comes to Juan Hsiao-ch'i's remark, "The life of man does not exceed one generation; the life of grass seldom lasts beyond autumn," [39] he cannot refrain from a touching, if somewhat exaggerated, discussion of the briefness of human life on earth in the manner of *Lieh-tzu*:[40]

As for man's life in this world, the longest is about seventy years. But this is very short indeed. Worse still, of these seventy years, half of them are nights. The days only occupy the other half. This is not all. Before the age of fifteen, we live in a state of ignorance. [These first fifteen years] should therefore be considered as lost to us. After the age of fifty, our ears and eyes gradually cease to function, and our backbones become stiff. [These last twenty years] should also be discounted. In between there are only thirty-five years, but even they are infested with wind and rain, disease and sickness, sorrow and worry, hunger and cold. . . .[41]

Life is not only short but troubled and unsatisfactory. "There is nothing," he says in his Introductory Remarks to Chapter 13, "that is not a dream: the earth itself is the country of Dream, past and present the shadows of dreams, honor and shame the stuff of dreams, and the mass of people the souls of dreams." [42] In such a world of illusions nothing, not even talent, strength, power, or favor can be relied on. So he writes in his Introductory Remarks to Chapter 31: "The Superior Man of old [knew that] talent cannot be depended upon forever, nor can strength, power, or favor. Although the world is big, there is in it nothing that can be depended upon forever. This is absolutely true." [43] His concern over the transitory nature of life prompted him to look toward a more ideal state of living where peace and tranquility were the rule. In a way typical of many Chinese intellectuals in a similar situation, Chin envisioned for himself an idyllic life in his forged preface to the *Shui-hu chuan*: a simple house by a river with tree-covered banks far removed from the centers of politics; a small plot of land to grow grain chiefly for wine; and a handful of good friends sharing the same tastes with him. The days are to be spent in conversation with friends on even the most trivial subjects, and at night, sitting alone under the lamp, he will write on subjects to his own liking. [44]

But he could never ignore the chaos which bandits were causing to the country in his time, and so took upon himself the task of attacking outlawry—the only way he could—in his commentary to the *Shui-hu chuan*. Such concern with the affairs of the day all but excluded him from the withdrawn quietist world he had elsewhere depicted.

II   *His Life under the Ch'ing (1645–1661)*

Chin was in his mid-thirties when the Ming empire fell before the invading Manchus. Like many other intellectuals of the period, he was deeply affected by this momentous political event. Whatever hope he might have entertained of holding government office before was now completely abandoned. He began to bury himself in books. "After the change of dynasty," his biographer Liao Yen records, "he gave up completely his hope for an official career. . . . Except for conversing with a few friends and followers, all he did was to sit alone in the Kuan-hua Study, engaged in reading and writing." [45] Chin wrote in a letter to his friend Wang Hsüeh-yi: "If Heaven will grant me twenty more years of life without sickness or worry so that I may cheerfully eat my food and annotate fully the few score old volumes in front of me, one by one, then I shall feel extremely grateful." [46]

Chin's decision to devote himself exclusively to reading and writing proved to be a happy one. For the first time he seems to have succeeded in some measure in leading the kind of private and secluded life described in his forged preface to the *Shui-hu chuan*. He now could pause and recall with perfect tranquility the happy things of his youth, some of which we have already seen above. He could find great pleasure looking at "a bird, a fish, a flower, a clump of grass, or even a bird's feather, a fish's scale, a flower petal, and a blade of grass."[47]

The first major writing project undertaken during this period was his commentary to the *Hsi-hsiang chi* which, according to the chronicle *Hsin-ch'ou chi-wen*, was completed in 1656. The old self-regard and urge to meddle in the text are still there. In Part II, Act III, for example, after expounding the subtleties of a passage, he suggests that the reader fill a goblet with wine and propose a toast first to Ying-ying, the heroine in the play, who utters the words, next to the author of the play, who wrote them, then to Chin himself who has expounded them, and finally to the reader who has the wisdom to enjoy them.[48] As in the case of the *Shui-hu chuan*, whenever he has a point to make, he does everything possible to drive it home, never balking at liberal emendations of the text itself.[49] However, there is now a leisureliness and calmness about this commentary as a whole which is not always found in the *Shui-hu* commentary.

This is a period in which Buddhist-Taoist influences on him were at the highest. Not only were his mode of living and appreciation of nature distinctly Buddhist-Taoistic in style, but, as we shall see later in Chapter 5, the whole *Hsi-hsiang* commentary is informed by an exciting and brilliant application of basic concepts found in both Buddhism and Taoism. He seems to have enjoyed the friendship of several learned monks of the time. At the end of his Introductory Remarks to Part IV, Act IV of the *Hsi-hsiang chi*, he stated that among those who would understand his interpretations were two Buddhist monks.[50] Among his surviving correspondence dating from this period are pieces addressed to eight other monks.[51] It is perhaps also during this period that he wrote many of his observations on Buddhism, Taoism, and the *Yi-ching* (*Book of Changes*).

In the second month of the year 1660,[52] one year before his tragic death, Chin was urged by his son Yung to analyze T'ang Regulated Verse of the seven-syllable type. He agreed, and before the year ended, some 595 poems by 145 authors had been commented on.[53] These were later assembled by his son and printed under the title *T'ang ts'ai-tzu shih chia-chi* (*A First Collection of Poems by Geniuses of T'ang*), implying that there would have been more such collections had he lived longer.

Some time before he embarked on his analysis of Regulated Verse, he had begun annotating Tu Fu's poetry,[54] with which, according to his cousin Chin Ch'ang, he had been fascinated ever since the age of fifteen.[55] The annotations, however, were never completed. Possibly prompted by Tu Fu's example as a loyal minister and conscientious censor who would risk his life admonishing the emperor, the old Confucian urge within him to play an active role in public affairs came alive again. He was still in the midst of writing the Tu Fu annotations when he became involved in a local incident for which he finally paid with his own life.

The incident is known in history as "The Case of Lamenting in the Temple" (*k'u-miao an*).[56] Jen Wei-ch'u, the newly appointed magistrate of Chin's hometown of Soochow turned out to be a tyrant more interested in pleasing his superiors and in personal gain than in the general welfare of the people. He not only imposed harsh measures on those who were late in paying taxes, but even sold public grain for personal profit. The people of Soochow, outraged by measures both harsh and illegal, awaited only the opportunity to make their grievances known.

The chance appeared when early in 1661 news of the death of Emperor Shih-tsu was announced throughout the country. To mourn the emperor, a ceremony was held in the official residence of the Prefect of Soochow, where officials of all ranks in Kiangsu Province gathered. Taking this opportunity to air the people's grievances, a hundred or more scholars, among whom was Chin, lamented in the local Confucian temple. They then sounded bells, beat drums, and marched in a group in the direction of the Prefect's official residence. On the way, more than a thousand people joined them, and together they shouted and demanded the resignation of Magistrate Jen. Chu Kuo-chih, Governor of Kiangsu, immediately ordered the arrest of the leaders and eleven students were seized on the spot. This time Chin was pushed away by the dispersing crowd and escaped arrest.

An informal trial was conducted forthwith and to the surprise of everyone present, Magistrate Jen confessed that he did what he had done because of pressure from the Governor himself. "I had been in office for only two months," he said, "and there was no way for me to get money. But the Governor pressed [me] for gifts, so I could only sell public grain." [57] For fear he himself would be involved in the incident, Chu changed the wording of Jen's confession and justified Jen's harsh measures under the pretext of military exigencies. At the same time, he sent a memorial to the newly enthroned K'ang-hsi emperor, stating: "The unruly scholars . . . formed groups of hundreds and thousands strong, and roamed about the street in an outrageous manner, greatly disturbing the spirit of the lately deceased Emperor. Their crime is great and their evil deeds extreme." [58]

The act of disturbing the spirit of the departed Emperor alone would have constituted an offense serious enough to be worth the attention of the central government. The Manchu authorities, however, had still other reasons to be alarmed by Chu's report. Just one year before, the refugee Ming government in southern China under the command of Cheng Ch'eng-kung (Coxinga) had again sent an armada to invade the north. Although Cheng was eventually defeated and driven back to Amoy, the Manchu government was particularly sensitive about riots or protests of any kind since they might be connected with Cheng's subversive activities. The K'ang-hsi emperor immediately dispatched special envoys to investigate and supervise the trial of the case. To avoid further arousing the resentment of the people of Soochow, Governor Chu contrived to have the case moved to Chiang-ning (modern Nanking), where two cases of treason connected with Coxinga's invasion were being tried.

During the trial which ensued, some more names were brought up before the authorities. This time Chin was not exempt. After repeated beating and torture, he and seventeen other defendants were pronounced guilty of "treason." For this reason they were sentenced to death together with 103 others found guilty in the Coxinga cases. Chin's property was also confiscated, and his family exiled. On the first day of the seventh month, upon hearing the sentence, Chin sent a letter home in which he wrote: "Having one's head cut off is a most painful thing. And the loss of all one's property is very sad. How strange that I seem to have come upon both these things so unintentionally! If there is an amnesty, we may still see each other again. Otherwise, I die." [59] To the end,

Chin felt he had done nothing to warrant such severe punishment.
The *Ku-miao chi-lüeh* gives the following account of the execution carried out on the thirteenth day of the seventh month:

> At the time of execution the place was encircled by armed soldiers
> and the Governor himself presided. During the seventh and ninth
> hours, the criminals were taken from the prison. Their hands were tied
> behind them, small flags were placed on their backs, and their mouths
> were stuffed with pieces of chestnut wood. Hustled [by soldiers on both
> sides] they were rushed through the street. Relatives and other spec-
> tators who tried to stand close were driven back by the handles of
> spears and the flat sides of swords. In a short while, the cannon roared,
> and the heads of the criminals fell to the ground. Armed soldiers ran
> in all directions, and the officials dispersed in fear. On the execution
> ground, there remained only the reek of blood and severed heads.[60]

The fear supposedly shown by the soldiers and officials is presumably the historian's shorthand way of indicating the unjustness of
the case.

Chin was a many-sided man. Some of his biographers, seizing
upon the eccentric aspects of his life, impressed by his elevation of
popular fiction and drama to the realm of high literature, and
moved by his unjust death, have pictured him as the sort of rebel
or "revolutionary-romantic" who is to be found at the barricades
wherever oppressive political authority is to be defied and social
taboos to be protested.[61] More recently, others, unsympathetic
with his attack on the bandit-heroes of *Shui-hu chuan* and other
things, have labeled him as "a reactionary" and "a spokesman of
the ruling class of the old feudalistic society." [62] Between these
two opposing interpretations, is it possible to reconstruct a more
balanced and unbiased view?

I have tried to indicate in this account of his life that Chin was
basically a Confucianist, though deeply influenced by Buddhist-
Taoist teachings.[63] To illustrate this point more fully, let me quote
two more passages from Chin's writings. In his Preface to Ch'ü
Yuan's *Li Sao* he writes: "A Superior Man reads in order to acquire learning; learns diligently in order to make right his wishes;
makes his wishes sincere in order to cultivate his person; estab-
lishes his person in order to achieve his [proper] function [in so-
ciety]; makes good use of himself in order to accomplish his tasks

[in society]; completes his tasks in order to recompense his parents." [64] The Confucianist Chin still saw the basic duty of man as lying in the sphere of social conduct—in cultivating oneself in order to be a useful member of society and a filial son. When he undertook to annotate Tu Fu's poetry in the last years of his life, he admired Tu Fu not only as a great poet, but also as a conscientious and loyal minister in the best tradition of Confucian statesmanship. Commenting on the seventh line in Tu Fu's "Staying at the Eastern Division One Spring Night" (Ch'un su Tso-sheng) which goes: "I have a memorial to present tomorrow morning," Chin wrote: "If later readers of this poem want to know what Mr. Tu said in his memorial, it certainly consisted of only the following words and no more: Think of the common people below, and of the emperor above. [He hoped that] those above would accept good advice and that those below would pledge their loyalty. Alas! How can the likes of this be comprehended by mumbling petty scholars?" [65]

Chin was, of course, not the Confucian scholar who could be satisfied by memorizing a few passages from standard texts for the purpose of succeeding in official examinations. More interested in following the spirit rather than the letter of Confucian teachings, he had both the courage and insight to apply his version of these teachings in areas of human experience seldom touched by others before him. His high praise of the *Shui-hu chuan* and the *Hsi-hsiang chi*, for example, is at least partly due to his extension of the meaning of one of Confucius's remarks about the *Book of Poetry*: "The *Book of Poetry* can inspire one's emotions." [66] "Confucius once remarked," Chin said, "that the *Book of Poetry* can inspire one's emotions. I say this is also true with fiction." [67] By this he seems to mean that the problem is not whether certain literary genres have greater intrinsic value, but rather whether they can perform a certain desired function. If they do, they should be considered masterpieces. By Chin's standard, both the *Shui-hu chuan* and the *Hsi-hsiang chi* eminently deserve to be ranked with the recognized classics.

In a way his own explanation of his courtesy name, Sheng-t'an (literally, "the sage sighs") serves as a good index to his own character. When asked what he meant by it, he said, "In the *Analects* the expression 'sighing deeply said' (*k'uei-jan t'an yueh*) occurs twice. In the case of Yen Yuan,[68] he was sighing for [Confu-

cius] the sage (*t'an sheng*); but in the case of [Confucius] sighing to agree with [Tseng] Tien it is the sage who himself sighed
(*sheng t'an*). Am I not of [Tseng] Tien's sort?" [69] Here again is
the distinctive element of Chin's arrogance in identifying himself
outright with a Confucian disciple. Significantly, however, of
Confucius's seventy some disciples he chose only Tseng Tien who,
in his distaste for politics and in his interest in pursuing a free and
individual life, was probably the least "Confucian" and the most
nearly "Taoist." What may be even more important is that Chin
implied that in what he said and did he felt he had the full en-
dorsement of the Master himself. Chin was, in short, neither an
iconoclast nor an ultraconservative. He was, if we may use such
an expression, an imaginative Confucianist.

CHAPTER 3

His Literary Theory

ONE important fact to keep in mind in our discussion of Chin's general theory of literature is that he was first and last a practical critic, a literary commentator, and not a literary theorist. His primary concern was not to present a comprehensive, coherent system about literature, but rather to provide some practical guide for the reader to appreciate the artistic achievements of the several works he undertook to analyze. Therefore, in piecing together the many critical ideas scattered in his correspondence, book prefaces, and commentaries of various kinds, our purpose is not so much to establish him as a systematic theorist as to enable the reader to gain a better and deeper understanding of his practice as a critic as a whole. To facilitate our discussion, we shall divide this chapter into three parts.

I *Literature as Self-expression*

By positing a framework of four coordinates—work, artist, universe, and audience, Professor M. H. Abrams in his classic *The Mirror and the Lamp* distinguishes four major critical theories in Western literary history: mimetic, pragmatic, expressive, and objective. For all its diversities and varieties, the expressive theory, the main concern of Abrams's book, poses and answers "aesthetic questions in terms of the relation of art to the artist, rather than to external nature (as with the mimetic theory), or to the audience (as with the pragmatic theory), or to the internal requirements of the work itself (as with the objective theory)." [1] Poetry, for example, is considered primarily as the "overflow, utterance, or projection of the thought and feelings of the poet." [2] (*Cf.* Wordsworth's well-known dictum: "Poetry is the spontaneous overflow of powerful feelings.") One important result of such a literary program is the reordering of the poetic kinds, and the elevation of lyric poetry to the very top of the literary hierarchy. "As the purest expression of feeling, lyric poetry is 'more eminently and peculiarly poetry than any other. . . .'" [3]

Interestingly enough, while the expressive point of view is fairly young in the history of Western theory of art ("for its emergence as a comprehensive approach to art, shared by a large number of critics, dates back not much more than a century and a half"),[4] in China it seems to be not only an important view but also one of the oldest. The legendary Emperor Shun (traditionally believed to have reigned 2255–2208 B.C.) is reported to have said, "Poetry expresses the *chih*." [5] Whether we take the "*chih*" to mean "will" or "heart's wish," [6] the idea of poetry as a form of expression is unmistakable. The idea was made even clearer in the so-called "Great Preface" to the *Book of Poetry*, traditionally attributed to Confucius's disciple Tzu-hsia (507–400 B.C.) but more recently believed to be the work of the Later Han scholar Wei Hung (*ca.* 25 A.D.). "Poetry," the Preface states, "is where the heart's wishes go. What lies in the heart is 'wish,' when expressed in words, it is 'poetry.' When an emotion stirs within one, one expresses it in words; finding this inadequate, one sighs over it; not content with this, one sings it in poetry; still not satisfied one unconsciously dances with one's hands and feet." [7] Because of the canonical status of the *Book of Poetry*, it is perhaps to be expected that such a definition of poetry as given in the Preface was to exert a tremendous influence on later critics. The views of Li Chih, the Yuan brothers, and Chin Sheng-t'an himself on the nature of literature in general, as we have seen above in the first chapter, could all be traced back directly to the Preface to the *Book of Poetry*. The innovation of these critics lies not so much in the formulation of a new theory as in making a fresh application of an old one. By expanding the expressive theory of art to cover all forms of literature, they were able to detect the worth of the then generally despised vernacular literature.

Chin's position as an expressive theorist is even more clearly shown in the following definition of poetry he gave in a letter to a friend:

Poetry is nothing extraordinary; it is only the words which rise from the heart and lie at the tip of the tongue, and which everyone cannot help longing to utter. The scholars, making use of the ten thousand volumes they have studied thoroughly in their lifetime, cut such words into forms and embellish them with elegance. That poetry possesses forms and elegance is a thing the scholars boast about as due to the skill of which they alone are capable. As for its original nature, it is simply the words that, rising from everyone's heart and lying at the tip of his tongue, force themselves to be uttered, and not a thing the scholars can boast about as due to their special skill.[8]

The key concepts here, as we have seen above in the case of Li Chih and Yuan Hung-tao, are spontaneity and sincerity. Poetry, in other words, must concern itself with spontaneous and sincere feelings.

Such being the case, Chin did not believe there was any poetry, or at least any good poetry, that was purely descriptive in nature. "I have said that in the fine poetry by the T'ang poets," he said, "there has never been one line that just describes the scenery." [9] This does not, of course, mean that there is no descriptive element in poetry. The point is rather: in a good poem the description of some object or scenery is never made an end in itself; it is merely a means by which the poet tries to convey what he thinks or feels inside. Thus Chin went on to say: "Since the *Book of Poetry*, all kinds of plants and trees, birds and beasts have been described [in poetry], and yet there hasn't been one line that is [purely] descriptive in nature. Therefore, it is said, 'Poetry expresses the *chih*, and *chih* is where the heart's wishes go.'" [10]

Chin's position as an expressive theorist was so absolute that, like William Hazlitt, he did not hesitate even to identify poetry with the very feeling itself.[11] Any sudden emotional outburst, he argued, even the cry of a baby, can be considered poetry: "Poetry is a sudden cry from the heart, which comes to everyone, even a woman or a child, in the morning or at midnight. Now, suppose here is a newborn baby whose eyes cannot yet turn and whose fists cannot yet stretch, but who, extending its arms and twisting its feet, utters a sound from its mouth. When I look at it carefully, I find this is really poetry." [12]

The identification of poetry with feeling leads Chin to a rather mystical view of poetry in general. To him, poetry existed even before the invention of writing itself. Thus he writes in a letter to a friend: "Yesterday I read your honorable letter which said that poetry existed before the written characters. This is just a statement, and yet when I heard it, it sounded like the roar of the dragon under the sea (so enlightening it was)!" [13] Not only did poetry exist before writing, it was in fact in existence from the very beginning of heaven and earth. So Chin continues in his letter: "I therefore thought: the characters invented by Ts'ang Ti were naturally the product of man through study and experience. As for poetry, it was indeed born with heaven and earth." [14] "Poetry," as he wrote in another context, "is the original sound (*yuanyin*) of heaven and earth." [15]

When the expressive theory became the dominant art theory in the West, the artist came to assume a position of central importance in esthetic considerations. The audience, which had hitherto occupied a prominent place in the scheme of the pragmatic theory, was pushed aside and almost totally neglected. According to the new theory, the artist's foremost duty was to be faithful to his own feeling and his own genius. The artist, in other words, became his own sole audience and "the generator of aesthetic norms." [16] "I never wrote one single line of poetry with the least Shadow of public thought," so Keats declared. And according to Shelley, "A poet is a nightingale who sits in darkness and sings to cheer its own solitude with sweet sounds. . . ." [17] One would expect similar statements from Chin, whose poetic theory in general, as we have just seen, resembles so much that of the expressive theorists of the West. Such, however, is not to be the case. Here again we see the deep-seated Confucian influence in Chin's thought as a whole.

As noted in the beginning of Chapter 1, Confucianism taught that literature ought to exert a moral influence on the reader. The implication of such a teaching is clear: the ultimate value of literature is not to be sought in the artist or in the work itself, but rather, as with the pragmatic theory in the West, in the useful influence it has on the audience. The audience, then, becomes a very important factor in the rendering of esthetic judgment. That the audience does not disappear completely from the poetics of Chin can be attested by the following statement of his: "In writing poetry, one must express what is felt sincerely in the heart and what is felt in common with others in the heart. It is because poetry expresses what is felt sincerely in the heart that tears can fall in response to one's brush-strokes; and it is because it expresses what is felt in common with others in the heart that it can make one's readers shed tears in response to one's utterance." [18]

Once the reader, or the audience, enters into the picture, the poet can no longer do things at his own will. Whether his purpose is to please or to teach or something else, he has to take into consideration someone other than just himself. He is no longer the sole "generator of aesthetic norms." According to Chin, the best course for the poet to follow, under the circumstance, is to observe the rule of moderation. In a statement strongly suggestive of the views of the well-known Confucian critic Shen Te-ch'ien (1673–1769) a few decades later, Chin says: "I have heard that moderateness, gentleness, sincerity, and deepness (*wen jou tun hou*) [are the qualities valued by] those who have a profound understanding of poetry. Isn't it that transparency, novelty, delicateness, and casualness (*ch'ing hsin chün yi*) have little to do with poetry?" [19]

If we call the expressive theorist a Romanticist and the pragmatic theorist a Classicist, from what we have seen above we may say that Chin Sheng-t'an was neither a pure Romanticist nor a thorough Classicist. Rather he was a Romanticist with the inclination of a Classicist. He was, in short, a Classicist-Romanticist.

II *Creative Process*

The shift of attention from the "universe" ("nature") and the audience to the artist himself in Western critical theory was accompanied, perhaps inevitably, by a great interest in the psychology of literary invention. Discussions and explorations of problems such as "inspiration," "imagination," "genius," etc., were conducted with a degree of intensity, seriousness, and rigor such as had never been seen before.[20] Since the expressive theory was not only one of the oldest, but also one of the most influential art theories in China, it is perhaps no surprise that similar problems should have attracted the attention of Chinese writers from early times. As early as the fourth century B.C., the philosopher Chuang-tzu had already shown in his parables of Cook Ting and Wheelwright P'ien[21] what one can achieve when thoroughly inspired and when one has completely mastered one's art. At the same time Chuang-tzu drove home the point that creation is something that can only be grasped intuitively, but not described in precise terms.

Both these points—the power and the mysterious nature of the

creative act—were elaborated on by later critics. In his famous
"Essay on Literature" (in rhyme), for example, Lu Chi (261–303)
states eloquently:

> Such moments when Mind and Matter hold perfect communion,
> And wide vistas open to regions hitherto entirely barred,
> Will come with irresistible force,
> And go, their departure none can hinder.
> Hiding, they vanish like a flash of light;
> Manifest, they are like sounds arising in mid-air.[22]

A little later, in a prose no less eloquent, Liu Hsieh (ca. 465–522),
author of the most comprehensive treatise on literature in Chinese, Wen-hsin tiao-lung (The Literary Mind and the Carving of
Dragons), writes of the power of imagination: "One who is engaged in literary thought travels far in spirit. Quietly absorbed in
contemplation, his thinking reaches back one thousand years; and
with only the slightest movement of his countenance, his vision
penetrates ten thousand li; he creates the music of pearls and jade
between his poetic lines, and he witnesses the rolling of wind and
clouds right before his brows and lashes. These things are possible
because of the work of the imagination." [23]

Essentially repeating what Chuang-tzu, Lu Chi, and Liu Hsieh
had said before him, but in his typically casual and unhurried
manner, Chin expressed his awe and fascination with the mysterious nature of creative writing: "The most extraordinary thing
about writing a composition is that the moment you spy with your
inward eye [what you are going to write], you immediately seize
it with your inspired pen. One moment earlier you were not able
to see it, nor will you be able to see it one moment later. As
though by mere chance and without any obvious reason you suddenly catch a glimpse of it at one moment in time. If you don't
grasp it then, you will never find it again." [24] To illustrate his
point, he draws two examples from everyday life. First, writing is
"like throwing dice. If you throw them a little too early or a little
too late, with or without force, slightly more toward the east or
slightly more toward the west, the outcome will not be the
same." [25] Second, writing is like the clouds in the sky, which
change from day to day:

I have often thought that since time immemorial, there has never been a day in which the sky is without clouds. Yet it has never happened that the clouds of today resemble those of another day. Why? Clouds are simply the vapors produced by mountains and rivers. As they ascend into the open air, and encounter light breezes, they are blown into thick patches. Since the wind has no fixed purpose, the clouds show no set patterns. Neither communicates with the other. They just happen to turn out this way. The [writing of] *Hsi-hsiang chi* is just like this. The author had neither purpose nor set pattern. It just happened that on a fine day sitting leisurely by the window he held a good pen with his dexterous wrist and suddenly without cause or reason it became like the wind tossing the clouds hither and yon. Had he tried it again at a different time, he might have achieved other extraordinary effects. But nothing can alter the fact that this time was a particularly great success. We need not insist [that a composition written at] another time cannot be better than [the one written at] this time. Nor need we say [that the composition written at] another time will necessarily be better than [the one of] this time.[26]

Chin's fascination with the mysterious nature of creative writing, however, did not prevent him from taking a closer and more analytical look at the mental process of the artist at work. In his commentary on the *Shui-hu chuan,* Chin praises the author's success in creating many highly individualized characters in the novel.[27] "If one paints several faces with one's hand," says he, "there are bound to be some that will appear like brothers. If one whistles several tunes with one's mouth, he is bound to repeat himself." [28] How then did the author succeed in creating so many diverse personalities? In Chin's effort to answer this question, he ventures on an extremely interesting discussion of the creative process of a great writer. He does this by the application of two cardinal Confucian precepts for conducting oneself and dealing with others, *chung* (loyalty) and *shu* (reciprocity).[29]

As Chin saw it, the secret of Shih Nai-an's success lay in his thorough acquaintance with the myriad things—both animate and inanimate—in the world. "For ten years," Chin says, "he (*i.e.* Shih Nai-an) investigated the nature of all things. Then suddenly one day all things had been fully investigated (*i.e.* became crystal clear)." [30] That is to say, Shih had finally arrived at a point where he felt completely at home with all the things in the world. But how did Shih Nai-an go about "investigating things"? Chin's answer is: by being aware of the existence of the principles *chung* and *shu*:

> The way to investigate things is through the principles of *chung* and *shu*. What is called *chung*? Everything in the world comes into exist-ence through certain causes (*i.e.* things are predestined to be what they are). Therefore, [once this fact is realized], we need not learn the principle of *chung* and yet we shall achieve it. Naturally everything in the world possesses the principle of *chung*. Fire possesses *chung*, my eyes possess *chung*, therefore what I see possesses *chung*. The bell possesses *chung*, my ears possess *chung*, therefore everything I hear possesses *chung*. Since I possess *chung*, other people also possess *chung*. Robbers and thieves possess *chung*. Dogs and mice possess *chung*. To realize the fact that robbers, thieves, dogs, and mice all possess *chung* is what we call the principle of *shu*. [Once the princi-ple of *shu* is also acquired], then things will be investigated, we shall be able to understand fully people's nature, and can even assist the transforming and nourishing powers of Nature and form a triad with Heaven and Earth.[31]

What Chin seems to be saying here is that everything possesses the principle of *chung*, which in his way of thinking seems to mean the way a thing is constituted—its "loyalty" or fidelity to its proper nature and its place in the scheme of things. Even a rob-ber, a thief, a dog, a mouse, or inanimate things such as fire or a bell are endowed with the principle of *chung*. Once we realize this fact, we will automatically acquire the principle of *shu*, which according to Chin's description seems to mean no more than a putting of oneself in the place of other things, thereby acquiring a perfect understanding of the way things are in the world. Once we achieve the principle of *shu*, we have succeeded in "investigat-ing the nature of things." We shall even be able to perform prodi-gious feats assisting the works of great Nature. Portraying 108 different individual heroes, therefore, is only a small test of Shih Nai-an's power as a creative writer since he succeeded so com-pletely in the "investigation of things." [32]

Indeed, Shih Nai-an can write on any type of character and bring him to life. In his Introductory Remarks to Chapter 55 Chin poses the question: "Nai-an was not himself a wanton woman or a thief. That is absolutely true. But when he writes about a wanton woman, she turns out to be truly one, and when he writes about a thief, the man is truly a thief. Why is this so?" [33] And his own answer: "If one is not a wanton woman, one certainly cannot know [what it is to be] a wanton woman. If one is not a thief, one certainly cannot know [what it is to be] a thief. When we say that Nai-an was neither a wanton nor a thief, we naturally mean Nai-an before he started to write. But once he employed his mind to become a wanton woman or as soon as he made up his mind to be a thief . . . he then became equally the one or the other." [34]

What Chin is trying to say here is really what a century and a half later Keats came to call "Negative Capability," a prerequisite for a good writer. A good writer, before he starts to write, is nothing but himself. But once his writing is under way, he loses his own identity and becomes part of what he creates. He must, in other words, have the ability to negate or lose his identity in something larger than himself. Or in Keats's own words: "As to the poetical Character itself . . . it is not itself—it has no self—it is everything and nothing—It has no character—it enjoys light and shade; it lives in gusto, be it foul or fair, high or low, rich or poor, mean or elevated—It has as much delight in conceiving an Iago as an Imogen." (Letter to Richard Woodhouse, Oct. 27, 1818.)[35] Shih Nai-an can portray vividly a wanton or a thief even though he himself had never been one precisely because he possessed (as did Shakespeare whose poetic character Keats was discussing) so thoroughly the "Negative Capability."

III *Form and Style—Chin's Concern with Literary Technique*

One common view held about the Romantic poets is that in their insistence upon spontaneous impulse as the essence of poetry they paid little attention to the technical side of poetry making, and that in the heat of their inspiration, they would dash off verses without thinking of form. Nothing, of course, is further from the truth. Wordsworth spent more than half his life revising the first version of *The Prelude*. And a look at the drafts of other Romantic poets shows clearly that even seemingly spontaneous lyrical poems achieved their final form only after some very painstaking revisions. However spontaneous and genuine (and therefore poetic) an emotion may be, it is not a poem unless it is adequately verbalized and formed. The very process of transforming an emotion into the concrete form of a poem involves artistic rules, whether explicit or implicit, which no poet can afford to ignore. Chin was apparently fully aware of this fact. For all his emphasis on spontaneous and sincere feelings, and the sudden sparks of inspiration which must be seized immediately, he did not overlook the importance of the technique of expression. In fact, going over his commentaries, one is struck by his preoccupation with the technique of writing. As we shall see later, it is precisely this preoccupation of his that helped him see excellent writing in two pieces of popular literature (*Shui-hu* and *Hsi-hsiang*), and this in turn prompted him to call them works of genius. Chin's overriding concern with technique also provides a focal point and a consistency to his commentaries which might otherwise appear merely collections of random jottings of impromptu thoughts.

Chin's emphasis on technique was based on the conviction that any good book must be the result of years of planning, meditating, and conscientious execution by its author: "When a man of the past wrote a book, he would often spend several years outlining it, several years accumulating the material, and another several years writing and rewriting it; only then would it be done, and come out in its full glory." [36] His definition of a genius further illustrates this conviction of his. To him, a genius is not someone who could turn out a piece of composition at an instant's notice, but rather someone who would work himself so hard that, so it would appear, "his heart stops, his breath is exhausted, and his face resembles that of a dead person." [37] Only then would what he writes appear effortless and unpremeditated. The apparent ease and instantaneousness with which Li Po was generally believed to have composed his poems, Chin further pointed out, are illusory. While he may have appeared facile and easy in the actual act of composing, the long preparation which led to this was a conscientious and arduous one.[38]

Chin's highest ideal in writing is *ching-yen* ("exquisite and strict"). "Any book in the world," he said, "that wishes to be placed in the Hall of Fame (*ming-shan*, literally 'celebrated mountains') and be handed down to later generations, must possess the quality of *ching-yen*. What is meant by *ching-yen*? It means that every word must have its principle of organization (*fa*); so must every sentence, every section, and every chapter." [39] Chin does not go on to make clear what he means by "principle of organization." However, since *ching* also suggests "fine," "essential," etc., and *yen* "urgent," "tight," etc., what Chin has in mind here is probably what he says later in his *Hsi-hsiang* commentary: "In writing a composition, there must not be one sentence or [even] one word which is brought in at random." [40] In other words, every little detail in a good piece of writing must be deliberated thoroughly, and be made to perform essential structural functions.

Here Chin was obviously under the influence of the rigid rules governing the composition of the so-called "eight-legged essay," the required essay form in the traditional civil service examinations.[41] In spite of its stifling effects on the intellectual life of China (how can any original and far-reaching idea be expounded within the limit of six hundred words or so—the prescribed length of the essay?), when viewed simply as a piece of literary composition, the eight-legged essay has at least the following two merits to recommend it: First, it teaches the writer how to write tightly woven compositions, in which each segment contributes substantially to the whole. Second, it forces the writer to write economically by presenting his main point without bringing in any unnecessary words. Both these points are implied in Chin's idea of *"ching-yen."* The deep influence the eight-legged essay had on Chin can also be seen in the fact that he would often use in his commentaries technical terms associated with the essay to discuss the literary merits of the various works involved.

Since a fine piece of writing involves such careful planning, what a reader should do, then, is not merely to entertain himself or to gather information. He must go to the heart of the matter and ponder the intricate ways by which the author expresses his ideas and feelings. Only then can he come close to appreciating the author's true spirit. This is exactly what Chin wanted to do with his various commentaries. He said of the *Shui-hu chuan*: "I am particularly disturbed at the thought that the reader's attention might not be kindled and the author's meaning, therefore, will be completely lost. If we don't appreciate the pains the author has taken, we will be turning our backs on fine craftsmanship. It is for this reason that despite my stupidity I have written the present commentary." [42] And in the case of the *Hsi-hsiang chi*: "In my comments on the *Hsi-hsiang chi*, I value only seeing eye to eye with the deceased author. I dare not evade too much [my responsibility as a critic]." [43]

Chin in fact had great expectations for his commentaries. He hoped they would serve as models, so that the reader would not only see the hidden excellences in the works involved, but also learn from them how to read other books. At the end of his Third Preface to the *Shui-hu chuan*, Chin says to his son Yung, and so to all readers:

I now . . . gladly pass on to you this copy of the book with my old comments in it, for I consider the writing contained therein to be of the first order of excellence. After you have read it, you will know how to read any book. If you can truly master the method . . . you may use it to read through all the books in the world as easily as splitting bamboo. Then you will sigh over the truth that Shih Nai-an's *Shui-hu chuan* is chief among all writings. Were it not for this commentary, you might be like other young men who would read through the book only casually—you would not only owe a debt to Shih Nai-an, but to me as well.[44]

Similarly, in No. 24 of the eighty-one notes he provided on how to read the *Hsi-hsiang chi*, he illustrates his point by telling a story of his childhood:

When I was young, I heard someone telling a joke. Once there was a man who suffered from extreme poverty. All his life, however, he had reverently worshiped the Taoist Patriarch Lü. Patriarch Lü, being touched by his piety, suddenly descended into his household. Upon seeing his utter penury, the Patriarch pitied him greatly, and thought that there must be some way to help him. Thereupon he pointed his finger at a huge rock in the yard, and the rock was transmuted into glittering gold. The Patriarch asked, "Do you want it?" The man bowed down once more and replied, "No, I don't want it." Patriarch Lü was delighted, and said, "Since you are so sincere, I now can teach you the Tao." The man replied, "No! No! What I really want is this finger of yours." At that time, I said to myself, "This is just a joke, that's all. If it had truly been Patriarch Lü, he would certainly have given his finger to the man." Now this *Hsi-hsiang chi* is the very finger of Patriarch Lü. Those who get it can find gold wherever they point.[45]

In his effort to set an example of how to go about appreciating a work of art, Chin helped to introduce something badly needed in Chinese literary criticism. In general, practical criticism in China seems to me to manifest an unfortunate tendency to indulge in mere abstract talk. A literary work is praised or condemned in terms so vague and general that little or no help is given us in our esthetic understanding of the work concerned. For example, Yen Yü (*fl.* 1200) in his celebrated *Ts'ang-lang shih-hua* (*Discussions of Poetry by Ts'ang-lang*) comments on the poetry of Juan Chi (210–263) thus: "After the reign (220–226) of Emperor Wen of Wei only Juan Chi's 'Yung-huai Poems' ('Poems Expressing Personal Feelings') are very lofty and ancient (*kao ku*), and possess the wind and bone (*feng ku, i.e.* spirit and style) of [the poets of] the Chien-an period (196–219)." [46] And on the poetry of Tu Fu (712–770) and Li Po (701–762): "Tzu-mei (*i.e.* Tu Fu) cannot do the free and romantic (*p'iao yi*) in T'ai-po (*i.e.* Li Po), and T'ai-po cannot do the solemn and melancholy (*ch'en yü*) in Tzu-mei." [47] After going over these passages, we are puzzled: we feel they have something important and interesting to say, but what that something is we do not know. What, for instance, does Yen Yü really mean by such high-sounding but vague terms as "lofty and ancient," "free and romantic," and "solemn and melancholy"? Unless Yen Yü goes one step further (which he doesn't) and demonstrates to us *in what way* the styles of the various poets concerned can be characterized by those terms, they will remain simply so many X's and Y's—high-sounding perhaps, but hardly helpful to our literary appreciation. When set against such abstract discussions, Chin's precise and detailed esthetic criticism is seen to possess special significance. By concerning itself primarily with the art of composition and the artistic function of individual words or expressions, the basic stuff that constitutes literature, it makes the discussion of literature much more than mere abstract talk.

Chin's emphasis on language and on the close scrutiny of a given text reminds us incidentally of the trend of the so-called New Criticism in recent Anglo-American literary criticism, which can best be characterized as an effort to make a literary work itself the primary object of literary study (Abrams's "objective theory"). In such a literary program, language naturally assumes a paramount importance. In the analysis of a poem, for example, what really matters is not how much of the poet's own personality or of the character of his time has been reflected in it, or how many allegorical meanings we can read into it, but rather how much we can find out about "the meanings, ambiguities, and interactions of the individual words, images, and passages." [48] To be sure, Chin, like the New Critic, is not without his limitations.

He would apply his basic critical approach indiscriminately to all forms of literature, be they drama, philosophy, or history, to the neglect of generic differences, or distinctive properties that can only be found in one form of literature, and not in another. Thus he said, "Originally I had selected six books which I call the Works of Genius. . . . Actually in reading these six books my basic method is the same. For example, when I read the *Hsi-hsiang chi*, I actually employ the same method as in reading the *Chuang-tzu* and *Shih-chi*. And even in reading the *Chuang-tzu* and *Shih-chi*, I employ the method used in reading the *Hsi-hsiang chi*. . . ."[49] The result is a leveling of the differences between the various genres, which finally led him to pronounce boldly that from the standpoint of the principle of composition (*wen-hsin*) only Chuang-tzu could have written the *Shih-chi* and only Szu-ma Ch'ien could have written the *Chuang-tzu*.[50] Moreover, the rigorous application of his approach would sometimes bar him from appreciating literary works which depend for their merits upon elements other than good writing and good organization, such as humor, satire, or merely an exciting story. The *San-kuo chih yen-yi* (*Romance of the Three Kingdoms*) and the *Hsi-yu chi* (*Pilgrimage to the West*, or *Monkey*) thus failed to meet his standard of literary excellence. He characterized these works in the following statement to which most critics today would certainly take exception:

In the *San-kuo* there are too many characters and events, and too much conversation. [As a consequence,] the author's pen cannot move or turn [at its will]. The whole thing is just like an official sending words through his attendant. The latter would only use his voice to announce what he has been told. Indeed, how dare he add or subtract a word? (Implying that the author is hampered by historical facts.) The *Hsi-yu*, on the other hand, is too fantastic. The author just made it up paragraph by paragraph. It is like the setting-off of fireworks on New Year's Eve, which pass by one group after another with no connecting link in between. When we read it, we can stop at any place.[51]

Yet in spite of these limitations, which are due more to the way he applied his method than to weaknesses inherent in the method itself, Chin, again like the New Critic in the West, has at least helped to provide a methodology through which meaningful discussions of literary works can be conducted.

CHAPTER 4

The Shui-hu *Commentary*

I *Synopsis of the Novel* [1]

*S*HUI-HU CHUAN, known to the West through the partial
translations of Pearl Buck (*All Men Are Brothers*) and J. H.
Jackson (*Water Margin*), is one of the most popular traditional
novels in China. Written in the vernacular language of the Yuan
and the Ming, it tells in 120 chapters of the exploits of a band of
108 lusty, courageous bandit-heroes of the twelfth century, and
how, under various circumstances, they one by one, and then in
groups, seek sanctuary at Liang-shan-p'o, a mountain lair in the
midst of a huge marsh. These bandits do not hesitate to attack the
wealthy and powerful and rob them of their ill-gotten property,
and to fight against government troops commanded by corrupt
and oppressive officials. For all their defiant actions, however,
deep in their hearts, especially in the heart of Sung Chiang, the
leader of the group, they still yearn for a chance to serve the Emperor and demonstrate their loyalty to him. In the end they are
pardoned by the Emperor, and being incorporated into the imperial army, take part in a series of campaigns against the invading
enemies from abroad and against other rebellious forces at home.
The campaigns are very successful, though the last one proves to
be rather costly, for more than half of the band of heroes die in
the course of it. Those who survive become further dispersed, and
the novel ends tragically with the death of Sung Chiang at the
hands of intriguing court officials.

II *Emendations of the Text*

The commentary on this novel was Chin's first major critical
activity. In a manner reminiscent of Chu Hsi's famed annotated
edition of *The Four Books*, Chin first wrote three prefaces in which
his reasons for the undertaking are explained, and the achieve-

ment of Shih Nai-an (the putative author of the novel) is
assessed. He next wrote "How to Read the *Fifth Work of Genius*"
which contains not only the kind of advice suggested by its title,
but also many critical comments on the literary achievement of
the novel as a whole. Beyond this prefatory material, a section of
Introductory Remarks is provided before each chapter, and within
each chapter critical comments are inserted between passages,
sentences, and frequently even words.

Chin's activity, however, is not confined to providing critical
comments.[2] It appears that wherever he deemed it desirable, he
did not hesitate to alter the text—the most drastic change being
the discarding of fifty of the hundred and twenty chapters.[3] That
is to say, the story from the second half of Chapter 71, where the
108 heroes are gathered at Liang-shan-p'o, to the end of the novel
is deleted. To bring the story to a conclusion, Chin composes an
episode where Lu Chün-yi has a vision of the execution of the
band, and this creation of his he attaches to the second half of
Chapter 71. Moreover, he combines the book's original Prologue
(*yin-tzu*) and Chapter 1 into a single chapter and calls them the
Induction (*hsieh-tzu*),[4] using a technical term from Yuan drama.
The earlier Chapter 2 thus became Chapter 1 in his edition, Chapter 3 became Chapter 2, and so on. For this reason, his version of
the novel is most often referred to by later scholars as the seventy-
chapter edition.

Whatever one may think of the drastic surgery applied to the
story, Chin's version, primarily because of his changes and emendations, is (a) more consistent, (b) more compact, and (c) more
vivid than that of his predecessor. Let us treat each of these im-
provements at some length.

A   *Consistency*

As demonstrated by Irwin in his *The Evolution of a Chinese
Novel*, the *Shui-hu chuan* in its early form is largely derived from
a number of story cycles which passed through a long process of
evolution, and its individual authorship has never been established beyond doubt.[5] In such a random growth, inconsistencies
in the narrative are inevitable. When Chin undertook to write the
commentary, as a good editor he eliminated a good many of them.
A sample of some of the more important ones will suffice here.

Chapter 54 of the older edition tells about the defeat of Kao

Lien and the rescue of Ch'ai Chin in a dry well by Li K'uei. The title of the chapter, however, reads (the italics are mine): "The Dragon of the Clouds (*i.e.* Kung-sun Sheng) uses magic to defeat Kao Lien. The Black Whirlwind (*i.e.* Li K'uei) *searches a cave* to rescue Ch'ai Chin." And in Chin's version (Chapter 53), the title is appropriately changed into: "The Dragon of the Clouds uses magic to defeat Kao Lien. The Black Whirlwind *descends a well* to rescue Ch'ai Chin." In Chapter 23 (Chin 22) Wu Sung is said to have drunk altogether fifteen bowls of wine before he started to cross the Ching-yang Ridge. Chin, however, changed the total number to eighteen, because this is the amount of wine Wu Sung consumed if we add up the number of bowls he actually de- manded in the wineshop. Wu Sung finally crosses the ridge, after killing a huge tiger with his bare fists. He then meets his brother and takes lodging in his house. After somewhat more than a month, unable to stand the bold advances made on him by his amorous sister-in-law (P'an Chin-lien), Wu Sung decides to move out. According to the early version this happened "sometime in the eleventh month." [6] To be exact, however, the time should be set a month later, *i.e.* sometime in the twelfth month, which Chin makes it in his version of the novel.[7] Similar to this is the change from "early spring" to "late winter" in Chapter 26 (Chin 25).[8]

B *Compactness*

A major contribution to compression is Chin's deletion of most of the incidental *shih* and *tz'u* verses used so abundantly in earlier editions of the novel. Such verses are common in the prose narra- tives of traditional Chinese vernacular literature. Whatever func- tion the verses may have had originally,[9] by the time of the *Shui-hu chuan* they had ceased to be a necessary part of the narra- tive. In the majority of cases, they are stereotyped descriptions of either the physical appearance of a person, or the natural sur- roundings of a place, so add very little to the progress of the main story. Chin's decision to delete them can be defended at least on structural grounds.[10]

Not only were verses cleared from the Chin version, but even whole passages which he felt were redundant or added nothing to the movement of the story were excised. A good example can be found in Chapter 26 (Chin 25). P'an Chin-lien, after she had murdered her husband, acted openly as Hsi-men Ch'ing's mis-

tress. The older edition relates P'an's and Hsi-men's new freedom
in the following way:

> Everyday she and Hsi-men Ch'ing would indulge themselves seeking
> pleasures upstairs. This was unlike the former times in Old Mother
> Wang's house when they could only do so surreptitiously. Now there
> was no one in the house standing in the way, Hsi-men Ch'ing could
> stay and sleep through the night at his will. *From this time on, Hsi-*
> *men Ch'ing would not go back home for three or five nights on end.*
> *The members of his household, both high and low, were also unhappy*
> *about this. Truly the charm of a woman can ensnare and ruin a man.*
> *When there is fulfilment, there is also bound to be disaster. There is a*
> *poem to the air "Partridge Sky" (Che-ku t'ien) commenting specif-*
> *ically on the problem of "the charm of a woman". Truly:*

> *Their lust is as vast as heaven but they themselves are not free;*
> *Deeply in love they are entwined together.*
> *With their minds bent on joys and pleasures of the day,*
> *Never would they have thought troubles are arising right within*
>   *the same walls.*
> *They covet pleasures,*
> *And indulge in leisurely pursuits;*
> *But a brave strong man has come to seek revenge.*
> *Recall, if you will, the affair between King Yu of Chou and his*
>   *favorite lady Pao-szu.*
> *It did not cease until blood was smeared on the Dragon Spring.*

> Let it be told that Hsi-men Ch'ing and that woman were seeking pleas-
> ures from morning to evening, and were indulging in songs and wine.
> After they were intimately acquainted, they cared little if the people
> outside knew it or not. Every one on the street knew of the matter.
> But they all feared this man Hsi-men Ch'ing as a wicked fellow and a
> bully, and nobody wanted to be involved in the matter.[11]

Apparently finding this passage long-winded and repetitious,
Chin did away with the italicized parts in his edition, making a
much more compact version as a whole.

C Vividness

Besides making the narrative more consistent and trimming
passages he considered superfluous, Chin frequently touched up
the older text for pure literary effect. Sometimes the process in-

volved no more than the substitution of a word or two. In the episode of Wu Sung's fight with the tiger (Chin 22), as Wu Sung climbed up Ching-yang Ridge, he began to feel hot from the effects of the enormous amount of wine he had just consumed in the wine shop (eighteen bowls, remember), so he took off the felt-hat and carried it on his back. In the older version: "He then carried (*pei*) his felt-hat on his back." [12] But Chin substitutes for the verb "carried," "whisked away" (*hsien*), and immediately a neutral, static description becomes charged with a live and dynamic quality: "He then whisked away his felt-hat to hang on his back." [13]

Sometimes, however, the process is more extensive. In Chapter 6 (Chin 5), for example, when Lu Chih-shen reports to the abbot of Hsiang-kuo Monastery in the Eastern Capital, the older version has the following: "Chih-shen first inserted the stick of incense in the urn, bowed his head three times, and then presented the letter [of recommendation to the abbot]." [14] Chin's version reads: "Chih-shen didn't know where to put the stick of incense. The reception-ist monk could hardly suppress his laughter, and inserted it in the urn for him. [After Chih-shen had] bowed his head three times, the receptionist monk called to him to stop. [Then Chih-shen] presented the letter [of recommendation to the abbot]." [15] The awkwardness of a rough and uncouth Chih-shen is deftly and amusingly captured in Chin's version.

The enlivening of dialogue is another aspect of Chin's editorial procedure. Lu Hsün has noted one example of this in his *A Brief History of Chinese Fiction* (pp. 193–94).[16] Let us cite one more for illustration. In Chapter 26 (Chin 25), Wu Sung has killed his sister-in-law to avenge his brother's murder. In his eagerness to find Hsi-men Ch'ing, the other adulterer, he seizes Hsi-men's chief clerk and questions him. In the older edition, the passage runs this way:

Wu Sung changed his expression and said, "Do you want to die or to live?"

The chief clerk was frightened and said, "Your honor, you are above me. This humble little person has never injured or offended your honor."

Wu Sung said, "If you want to die, don't tell me where Hsi-men Ch'ing has gone. If you want to live, tell me truthfully where he is."

The chief clerk said, "He has just gone with a friend to the wine shop under the Bridge of the Lions to drink wine."

As soon as Wu Sung heard this, he turned and went away.[17]

And here is Chin's version with the differences italicized:

Wu Sung *suddenly* changed his expression and said, "Do you want to die or to live?"

The chief clerk was frightened and said, "Your honor, you are above me. This humble little person has never injured or offended your *hon . . . !*"

Wu Sung said, "If you want to die, don't tell me where Hsi-men Ch'ing has gone. If you want to live, tell me truthfully where he is."

The chief clerk said, "He has just with . . . *with* . . . a friend gone to . . . *to* . . . the wine shop under the Bridge of the Lions to drink . . ."

As soon as Wu Sung heard this, he turned and went away.[18]

The superior theatricality of Chin's version is evident. The word "suddenly" is added before "changed" in segment one; the clerk is twice stopped short in his speech (once at the end of segment 2 and once at the end of segment 4); and the clerk's fright is shown by his speaking with a stammer. As a result of these changes, what was once a rather matter-of-fact dialogue is transformed into a lively and dramatic exchange.

Sometimes for the sake of a more arresting situation, Chin would even change the content of the story. In Chapter 63 of the Chin version, for example, Hsüan Tsan, the Ugly Warrior, is made to suffer capture by Third Daughter Hu, a woman warrior, rather than by another man, Ch'iu Ming, as is the case in the older edition. The reason is not difficult to see. Hsüan Tsan, an uncouth-looking fellow, was nicknamed the Ugly Warrior, so to have him captured by a handsome woman makes a piquant contrast. Thus Chin writes in his comment after the incident in the story: "A woman warrior is specially added here in order to make the three characters *ch'ou chün-ma* ('Ugly Warrior') stand out more prominently." [19] Changes affecting situations that belong to the tradition, however, are very rare.

In many of the additions, deletions, and changes we have seen thus far, Chin can be faulted, of course, for introducing elements alien to a work that evolved out of an oral tradition. Although more vivid and compact in style, Chin's version was even further removed (than its predecessors) from the story as told by the storyteller with its characteristic looseness and repetitiousness.

D *The Deletion of the Last Part of the Story*

The most drastic change Chin made in the *Shui-hu chuan,* as already noted above, is the discarding of the second half of the traditional story. We shall have occasion in the next section to discuss the motives behind such an act. For the moment, let us view it purely from an esthetic point of view. In other words, all things being equal, is Chin's effort esthetically justifiable in the same sense that the revisions we have just seen may be claimed to be?

Sympathetic critics of Chin have commented that there is a marked decline in literary quality in the story beyond Chapter 71. Irwin makes this point clear when he writes: "Quite apart from the inferiority of the interpolated passages, there is a definite falling off in the calibre of the Shih Lo version (*i.e.* the 120-chapter edition) once the heroes have assembled. Henceforth it was bound to depict them, for the most part, as acting in a group rather than as individuals; and except for occasional flashes of inspired writing . . . the falling action fails to attain the artistic level of the early episodes." [20] Such a consideration, though not without some weight, is not justification for what Chin did to the original story. Apart from the elementary consideration that we as readers of an exciting story would naturally wonder what happens once the 108 heroes gather in Liang-shan-p'o, Chin's truncation has destroyed the basic design of the novel as a whole. Although episodic in structure, the novel is yet informed by "a magnificent literary conception" as Shih Nai-an builds "his material up into a great mass tragedy. The rebels are successful so long as they do not make peace with the court and are not pardoned; then they die off one by one." [21] Irwin feels this difficulty with Chin's version too as he goes on to say, "On the other hand, did he (*i.e.* Chin Sheng-t'an) not realize that the underlying unity of the story was as truly a feature of its greatness as the details of presentation? For the sake of preserving that unity he might have been content to leave that text unchanged, since his own talents were clearly not sufficient to improve upon it." [22] As Lu Hsün succinctly puts it, the final impression we get from reading Chin's version of the novel is like seeing "a dragonfly with a broken tail." [23]

E   *The Propriety of Tampering with the Text*

An inevitable question connected with the discussion of Chin's changes of the text is that even though those changes can most of the time be justified from an esthetic point of view, can they also be justified on ethical grounds? In other words, what right did Chin have to tamper with the work of someone else, however superior his own literary taste may have been? One explanation for this is that, as we have noted in Chapter 1, fiction and drama were not highly regarded in traditional China, and for this reason they were often treated as something trivial, and anyone could do anything he wished with them. Different editors of different periods had all done their share in changing a text where they felt like it. A mere glance at all the variant readings of different editions at the end of each chapter of the variorum edition of the *Shui-hu chuan* (*i.e.* the *Shui-hu ch'üan-chuan*)[24] should confirm this assertion. This is also why, as evidenced by Irwin in his study of the *Shui-hu chuan,* the problem of variant editions occupies a prominent place in the discussions of traditional fiction and drama in China. Lu Hsün's remark in his essay "The Historical Development of Chinese Fiction" is pertinent here: "I suppose it is because the Chinese have always considered works of fiction trivial, unlike the Confucian classics, that they cannot help making alterations." [25] In this connection, it is illuminating to note that in his commentary on Tu Fu's poetry Chin never willfully changed the text involved. Scholars since Chin's time have discussed the rights and wrongs of his revisions for a number of reasons, but none have ever questioned his "right" to make such revisions.

III   *Ambivalent Attitude toward the Bandits*

Going through Chin's *Shui-hu* commentary, the reader is struck by his oscillation between two opposing poles: his sympathy with the individual bandit-heroes on the one hand and his condemnation of outlawry on the other. Since the whole tenor of the commentary is colored by this ambivalence, unless we have some understanding of it from the beginning, we shall be at a loss to comprehend Chin's sometimes contradictory critical remarks.

The novel makes it clear that the 108 heroes are not born bandits; they are in many cases forced into banditry by an unjust society. Chin observes: "This lengthy book which consists of seventy chapters is going to write about 108 men. The reason the author first writes about Kao Ch'iu but not the 108 men is because if he started immediately writing about the 108 men without first writing about Kao Ch'iu, it would mean that disorder is produced from below. In fact the author, before writing about the 108 men, first tells us about Kao Ch'iu: this is a case of disorder being generated from above." [26] Kao Ch'iu is a young good-for-nothing whose sole ability in life is his skill at kicking a football. The story of his rise from an idler to the post of Minister of War (*t'ai-wei*) epitomizes the corrupt nature of the government. By beginning the novel with a story of Kao Ch'iu, Chin implies, the author is foreshadowing the inevitable later consequences. Chin's feelings become clearer in his Introductory Remarks to Chapter 51: "Alas, I can hardly suppress my sorrow and tears when I see how Kao Lien, on account of his cousin Kao Ch'iu's power and influence, does whatever he wishes in the local government, and how Yin Chih-ko, further by means of the power and influence of Kao Lien, his brother-in-law, does whatever he pleases in the town." [27] And when Yin Chih-ko's actual crime is recounted, Chin's comment runs as follows:

Kao Ch'iu does what he wishes; but there is still some limit to it. But how can there be a limit to what his cousins wish to do? . . . Moreover, his cousins also have relatives who in turn do whatever they wish. . . . The relatives again have their own dupes who in turn do whatever they wish. . . . Alas, the world is the emperor's property, and the people in it his children. Now he lets loose these unrestrained tigers and wolves whose desires are insatiable . . . and yet he desires people not to rebel and the state to be imperishable—how can this be? [28]

Chin often expresses very strong sympathy for those heroes whose misfortunes are the direct results of the evil official system exemplified by Kao Ch'iu and his followers. In Chapter 11 (Chin 10), after Lin Ch'ung points out the wrongs Kao Ch'iu has done to him, Chin writes by way of comment: "Every word is a teardrop, and every tear is a drop of blood. I can hear his voice even today." [29] Chin not only felt sympathy for the heroes but admired some of them greatly. Li K'uei, the Black Whirlwind, is described as "a man of genuine feelings, at once admirable and lovable," [30] and Wu Sung is a "Heavenly Human" (*t'ien-jen*).[31]

At the opposite extreme we find Chin bitterly condemning the bandits as a group. In his Second Preface to the novel, he calls them "malignant" and "evil" things to be attacked and despised by all men.[32] He takes exception to the attributes *chung* (loyal) and *yi* (righteous) that editors before him had prefixed to the title of the novel: "Loyalty is the greatest rule for serving one's superiors, and righteousness the highest principle for ordering one's inferiors. . . . Now if loyalty and righteousness are supposed to be found in the 'Water Margin,' must they not be the most evil and malignant things in the world?" [33]

When condemning the bandit-heroes as a group, Chin singles out Sung Chiang, the leader, for special attack. In "How to Read the *Fifth Work of Genius*" he writes: "*Shui-hu chuan* contains much serious writing. However, its author's detestation of Sung Chiang is extreme. . . . The reason the author of the *Shui-hu chuan* singles out Sung Chiang is because he intends to destroy the chief rebel. The rest are forgiven." [34] To prove his point, Chin never loses a chance in his commentary to paint Sung Chiang black.[35] The tone of Chin's attack on Sung is set in the Introductory Remarks to Chapter 17:

In this chapter we begin to touch on the biography of Sung Chiang. Sung Chiang is the chief of the bandits, and for this reason his crime is one degree greater than the others. It has ever been the case, however, that readers of *Shui-hu* often overpraised Sung Chiang's loyalty and righteousness, as though they would like to meet him any day or night. This is not because they would like to be friends with the bandits— they simply cannot comprehend the hidden meaning of what they read. In my view, the reason Sung Chiang's crime is greater than that of the other bandits is less because he wrote a seditious poem than because he set Ch'ao Kai free. Why? After Ch'ao Kai was freed, he led and assembled various dissidents, and brought disorder to the imperial court. [The whole trouble] started from here. If Sung Chiang had been a loyal and righteous man, he certainly would not have freed Ch'ao Kai. It follows then that since Sung Chiang did free Ch'ao Kai, he could not have been a loyal and righteous one. This is the beginning of Sung Chiang's biography. But the author first writes nothing but how Sung secretly set Ch'ao Kai free. So this immense crime of Sung Chiang's even the author cannot conceal for him.[36]

Everything Sung does is seen in a distorted, unfavorable light. In the novel, for example, Sung is always a generous man with his money. According to Chin's line of argument, however, this is only a means by which Sung buys himself a good name. Chin's most frequently used epithet for Sung is "opportunistic" or "scheming" (*ch'üan-cha*). Once more he made numerous changes to bolster his contentions.[37]

Despite Chin's monumental effort to blacken Sung Chiang, the original Sung Chiang shines through clearly in spots, and there are sometimes ridiculous discrepancies between the false and wicked Sung Chiang found in Chin's commentary and the faithful, generous-hearted Sung Chiang implied by the attitudes and words of other characters in the novel.[38]

But Chin's greatest condemnation of the bandits as a group lies in his discarding of the final portion of the novel—constituting more than a third of the story. In the older edition of the novel, after the 108 heroes have assembled at Liang-shan-p'o, they are finally pardoned by an Imperial edict, and are enlisted in the service of the country. Chin greatly resents this, and enumerates eight reasons why outlawry cannot be encouraged and the bandits must never be pardoned.[39] To make certain others are not tainted, he simply stops the story at its climax and invents a dream scene in which the entire group is summarily executed by an Imperial envoy. "You violent robbers who deserve ten thousand deaths," roars the Imperial envoy. "You have committed crimes that fill the universe. . . . If I pardon you today, what law could be invoked to rule the world hereafter?" Here Chin hastens to add in his commentary: "This is a deathless statement!" [40] Just as he is to be executed, Lu Chün-yi, the dreamer, looks up, trembling, and sees a tablet on top of the hall, on which are written four big characters saying, "Universal peace throughout the world." And Chin's comment here is: "These truly are auspicious words!" [41]

Why should there be this violent and sometimes grotesque ambivalence in Chin's feelings about the novel? Two views have been advanced. Hu Shih argues that Chin was writing at a time when the country was torn apart by two bands of outlaws, led by Chang Hsien-chung (1605–1647) and Li Tzu-ch'eng (1605–1645). Having seen the havoc they caused—which contributed in no small degree to the downfall of the Ming Dynasty—Chin deeply believed that outlawry should not be shown in an accept-

able light even in fiction.⁴² The second view also goes back to history for an explanation: Because of the obvious glorification of
brigandage in the novel, Emperor Szu-tsung of Ming (reigned
1628–1643), whose rule was threatened by the roaming bandits,
issued an order banning the book's circulation. In order to rescue
the book, Chin is supposed to have tried to camouflage it by
changing the intention of the original author from one of glorification to one of condemnation of the bandit-heroes.⁴³

The second of the two views is rather farfetched. Chin's condemnation of outlawry in general is a bit too sincere to be that of
someone doing camouflage work. Further, Emperor Szu-tsung's
decree was promulgated on the twenty-third day of the sixth
month of 1642,⁴⁴ more than one year after the completion of
Chin's commentary. Timing alone invalidates the theory.

Of the two the first is the more plausible, because it agrees well
with Chin's philosophy as a whole. As already shown in Chapter 2
above, Chin was fundamentally a Confucianist, but was deeply
influenced by Buddhist-Taoist teaching.⁴⁵ The Taoist part of him
advocated natural development for each individual in society. So
he writes in his *Yü-lu tsuan* (*A Compilation of the Records of
Sayings*): "The sage makes no distinctions between the myriad
things in the world; he will let all of them develop their own nature fully. He will let all men in the world be happy or angry as
they wish." ⁴⁶ When applied to the sphere of political thought, this
means that: "A great ruler does not want to put himself in a position of director, but would rather let all the people in the world
direct things. He would love what they love, and hate what they
hate. This is what is called letting the good originate with
Heaven. And Heaven is simply a term for the people." ⁴⁷ If the
ruler does not let the people do what their nature dictates, there
will be disorder and chaos: "People at the end of a dynasty, under
pressure exerted by the king from outside, dare not express their
feelings fully; and yet being forced by their nature from within,
they must express their feelings fully. As a result, they will deceive
the king . . . form intriguing parties and accuse each other
falsely . . . murder their fathers and assassinate their lords.
. . ." ⁴⁸ The story of the 108 bandit-heroes in the *Shui-hu chuan*
Chin took to be a case in point. "Alas," says Chin in his
Introductory Remarks to Chapter 2, "the bandits' talents are suit-
able to serve at court and their strength is suited to fight on the

battlefield, but they are forced one and all to enter the lair. Whose fault is it?" [49] Therefore Chin shows strong sympathy for the individual heroes (always of course excepting Sung Chiang).

But he was a Confucianist. He could not advocate the abolition of government as Lao-tzu and Chuang-tzu would. No matter how important a position the common people occupy in Chin's political thinking, high above them in Chin's mind there still rules a king—who should of course be an enlightened and benign king. The king is not just a person who commands the people's respect and obedience; he is the pivot of social order which must be kept intact at all times. "The former kings formulated the principle of propriety, which may never be destroyed though ten thousand generations pass," [50] says Chin. Though he feels sympathy for the misfortunes that befall many of the heroes, when their activities go beyond the bounds of what he sees as basic social propriety and they openly defy orders from the Emperor, Chin's reaction is bitter.

Alas, the Superior Men of old were all cautious and careful [in what they wrote] before their works were able to survive. *Shui-hu chuan* runs to hundreds of thousands of words and yet it ends with the words, "universal peace throughout the world." How clear is the author's intention! Later editors, however, had this section cut out, praised the imperial pardon, and tried their best to place the blame on the court and attribute the merit to the robbers. They even openly prefixed the terms "loyal" and "righteous" to the title. How could they be so intent on offending the ruler and creating disorder! [51]

IV *Appreciation of the Novel as a Work of Art*

Chin's uncompromising attitude toward outlawry, however, did not prevent his appreciation of the true value of the novel as a great work of art. He was able to maintain a clear distinction between the moral content of a work on the one hand and its artistic achievement on the other (something rare among traditional critics), for he writes in his Third Preface to the novel:

The *Shui-hu chuan* tells a story about 108 men. They are all highwaymen, and their profession is robbing and killing: they have lost the moral standards [they grew up with] and their consciences are blunted, and of course they are unworthy of emulation. But I insist on charting

the general development of the story and elucidating its spirit and style
(*shen li*) because this book . . . , if we focus our attention on its spirit
and style, will be discovered to be just like one or two sections from the
Analects—transparently clear, shiningly bright, pleasantly light, and
glitteringly fresh. Does this not put it in the same high class as *Chuang-
tzu* and *Shih-chi*? Otherwise how could it be like this? If one must condemn the content of a book because of its story, then of the "Airs of
the States" (a section in the *Book of Poetry*) half of them are licentious
and tainted, and nine tenths of the *Spring and Autumn Annals* concerns assassination and usurpation. But I do not hear that people would
dispense with the sacrificial vessel because they detest evil spirits and
demons, or that they would kill [the good historian] Yi-hsiang because
they detest the unpleasant stories he recorded. This concept is extremely clear and easy to comprehend.[52]

Chin had, in fact, the highest praise for the literary achievement of the novel. "Of all the literary works in the world," he
wrote, "none can surpass the *Shui-hu chuan* in excellence." [53] Even
Szu-ma Ch'ien's *Shih-chi*, the *Third Work of Genius* which Chin
thought would "survive ten thousand years without a rival (*tu pu
wan nien*)," [54] looks pale beside the *Shui-hu chuan*: "All the devices used in the *Shui-hu chuan* are taken from the *Shih-chi;* yet
the former surpasses the latter in many places, while all the very
best aspects of the *Shih-chi* can all be found in the *Shui-hu
chuan*." [55] And the reason for this, as Chin saw it, is that Szu-ma
Ch'ien was writing history, and so was hampered by his material;
Shih Nai-an was mainly creating a story in his mind, and so could
do whatever he wanted with his material.[56] This shows an understanding of the value of imaginative writing that few had
achieved before him.

Three things which Chin seems to have admired most about the
Shui-hu chuan are: (a) the characterization, (b) the vivid description of events, and (c) the technical virtuosity.

A   *Characterization*

In his comments on the novel, Chin is frequently fascinated by
the author's power to create vivid and lively characters. "*Shui-hu*
tells a story of 108 men: yet each has his own nature, his own
temperament, his own outward appearance, and his own voice." [57]
In another place, "When the book deals with the dispositions of
the 108, there are truly 108 different kinds of dispositions. In other

books, the people they describe will all look the same, be they as
many as a thousand or as few as two." [58] In the description of
rough men alone, for example, several kinds of roughness can be
differentiated in the novel. "The roughness of Lu Chih-shen,"
Chin writes, "is hastiness of disposition (*hsing chi*); that of Shih
Chin is the intractability of youth (*shao-nien jen ch'i*); that of Li
K'uei is barbarity (*man*); the roughness of Wu Sung is that of an
unrestrained hero (*hao-chieh pu shou chi-ti*); the roughness of
Juan Hsiao-ch'i comes about because of his suppressed sorrow
and anger (*pei fen wu ch'u shuo*); and the roughness of Chiao
T'ing is simply his evil disposition (*ch'i-chih pu hao*)." [59] It is precisely this highly successful creation of lively and individualized
characters that makes the *Shui-hu chuan* such fascinating reading: "Other books we read through once and stop. But the *Shui-
hu chuan* we never tire of reading; and all because it succeeds
completely in bringing out the different dispositions of all 108
men." [60] We do not have to agree with Chin in maintaining that
each of the 108 heroes is a highly individualized character. But
Chin's contention is at least partially true in that many of the main
characters in the novel are vividly portrayed.

B *Vivid Description of Events*

Chin expressed his admiration for the novel's vivid dialogues
and lifelike descriptions of events by the constant use of expressions such as "like a picture" (*ju-hua*), "a lifelike picture" (*huo-
hua*). In Chapter 37 (Chin), where Sung Chiang first meets Li
K'uei and Tai Tsung, for example, he uses one or another of these
expressions twenty-three times. The whole of Wu Sung's encounter with the tiger in Chapter 22 (Chin) is appreciated in terms of
painting:

I have often thought that there are places to see a painted tiger, but
none to see a genuine one; one can see a genuine tiger that is dead, but
not one that is living; a living tiger walking can probably be seen occasionally, but a living tiger battling with a man—there are never places
to see such a thing. Now suddenly in an almost casual way, Nai-an
with his pen has painted a complete picture of a living tiger battling
with a man. From now on those who want to see a living tiger can all
come to the Ching-yang Ridge in the *Shui-hu chuan* to stare to their
satisfaction. . . . I really don't know where in his mind Nai-an obtained this method of painting a tiger eating a man. When I say that of

all writers of the past three thousand years he alone is a genius, is this
mere empty praise? [61]

C Technical Virtuosity

But what impressed Chin the most about the novel was the skill
of Shih Nai-an as a writer, his mastery of a number of technical
devices. His admiration for this is indicated in such expressions as
"marvelous" (miao) or "marvelous writing" (miao-pi), and "unusual" (ch'i) or "unusual writing" (ch'i-wen), which are even
more liberally used than the "picture" comments.

He deplored anyone who regarded the Shui-hu chuan merely as
a collection of exciting stories to be read and remembered only as
something to talk about in social gatherings. "I hate those young
people of other families," he said, "who when they read a book
will ignore the art of writing. As long as they have committed to
memory a few incidents in the book, they consider themselves to
have read it. Since even the Chan-kuo ts'e and the Shih-chi are
passed over as collections of incidents, how much the more has
this been true of the Shui-hu chuan." [62] To help the uninitiated
appreciate the subtle art of the novel, Chin points out fifteen techniques used by Shih Nai-an. In order not to burden the reader
with too many unnecessary details, I will simply translate the
names of the techniques, sometimes accompanied by Chin's own
explanations, and then discuss them in modern critical terms: [63]

1. Prestatement (tao-ch'a fa). What Chin means by this technique is that important names or events to be treated at length
later in the story are first mentioned briefly so as to prepare the
reader psychologically. Of the four examples mentioned by Chin,
the one that can be most readily understood is that of Old Mother
Wang. Old Mother Wang operates a tea shop next door to the
house of Wu Ta-lang (Wu the First), Wu Sung's elder brother
and the husband of the ravishing P'an Chin-lien. Through Mother
Wang's efforts and maneuvers an illicit relationship is formed between P'an and Hsi-men Ch'ing, a wealthy local bully. Later, at
her suggestion and partly with her help, P'an murders Wu Ta-
lang by poisoning him. This leads to Wu Sung's revenge, which
constitutes some of the bloodiest and most exciting scenes in the
novel. Old Mother Wang can thus be said to have performed an
important role in the story. But before she enters the scene in the
second half of Chapter 23, her name is twice mentioned by P'an

Chin-lien in connection with the tiger seen at the beginning of the chapter. This alerts the reader's attention.

2. Inserted speech (*chia-hsü fa*). "This means that two people in great haste want to speak at the same time. It cannot be that after one has finished speaking, the other then begins. The author must write the speeches [so it seems] with one stroke of his pen (*i.e.* simultaneously)." The example given by Chin is from the episode in which Lu Chih-shen is traveling from Mt. Wu-t'ai to the Eastern Capital, and on his way comes upon two rascals disguised as monks at the Wa-kuan Monastery (Chapter 5). The full text of Lu Chih-shen's exchange with one of them is translated in Lu Hsün's *A Brief History of Chinese Fiction* (pp. 193–94) as follows:

> The monk (*i.e.* Ts'ui Tao-ch'eng) was startled when Lu Chih-shen came up. Jumping to his feet he said, "Please take a seat, brother! Have a cup with me."
> Grasping his wand, Lu demanded, "Why did you give up the monastery?"
> The monk said, "Sit down, brother, and let me . . ."
> "Out with it! Out with it!" Lu glared.
> ". . . tell you. In the old days our monastery was a fine place: plenty of land and many monks. But . . ." [64]

The effect of "simultaneous speech" is thus gained by the insertion of Lu Chih-shen's menacing "Out with it! Out with it!" in the midst of the monk's second speech. Unhappily, as pointed out by Lu Hsün (*Brief History*, p. 193), this effective stylistic device was not that of the original author, but rather Chin's own contribution.

3. The grey line of a grass snake (*ts'ao-she hui-hsien fa*). What Chin means by this technique seems to correspond partially to a fashionable phrase in modern criticism—the "recurrent image." That is to say, through the repetitive but unobtrusive use of a key image or symbol the author succeeds in achieving a unity or a certain purpose in his work similar to that achieved in a symphony through the recurrence of a motif. The most notable example is the author's effective use of the "club" image throughout the Chiang-yang Ridge scene, where Wu Sung subdues a huge tiger singlehandedly (Chapter 22). The whole episode, together with Chin's running comments, is translated in Section V below.

4. Writing with sweeping strokes (*ta lo-pi fa*). Chin does not give a clear account of what he means by this. By going through the examples enumerated, however, we may infer that he probably means a direct, forceful, even grandiose style. One example is the episode of Wu Sung's fight with the tiger already mentioned above and to be translated in full in the next section.

5. Pricking with a cotton[-wrapped] needle (*mien-chen ni-tz'u fa*).[65] In Western critical terms this technique is what might be called "satire." Both examples given by Chin are related to Sung Chiang, and according to Chin's own interpretation they are the means by which the author subtly managed to expose the wickedness in Sung Chiang's character—another illustration of Chin's prejudice against Sung Chiang. The full story of the first instance mentioned here goes this way: One day in a fit of temper Sung Chiang killed Yen P'o-hsi, a singing girl whom he had taken as mistress. As a result of this crime, he was later arrested, branded, and exiled to Chiang-chou. On his way to Chiang-chou he and his two guards were stopped by his bandit friends of Liang-shan-p'o. After taking him to the mountain lair, they begged him to join the band. Unwilling to disappoint his father who had repeatedly admonished him never to become a bandit himself, he declined the invitation and to show his firmness, when Hua Jung insisted Sung Chiang have his cangue opened, he stopped him saying, "What kind of talk is this, my worthy brother? This is a law of the country. We dare not touch it without authorization."[66] Later on, however, in Chapter 36 when Sung Chiang (continuing his journey to Chiang-chou) was resting in a house for the night, at the suggestion of the two guards Sung agreed to have his cangue opened. Chin comments: "When this passage is read against what has happened on Liang-shan-p'o earlier in the story, [we can see] that it is meant to reveal the craftiness (*ch'üan-cha*) of Sung Chiang."[67]

The second example concerns the death of Ch'ao Kai, the original leader of the band at Liang-shan-p'o. Each time Ch'ao Kai proposed to lead an expedition, he was dissuaded by Sung Chiang on the grounds that he was their leader and should not be risked, and someone else (usually Sung Chiang himself) would go in his place. In Chapter 59, however, Sung Chiang did not try to keep Ch'ao Kai from leading an expedition against Tseng-t'ou Shih, and Ch'ao Kai died from an arrow wound. Thereupon Sung

Chiang became the new leader of the band. Chin lays the blame for Ch'ao's death on Sung Chiang, implying that the latter had foreseen the outcome of the expedition! In the older edition, Sung Chiang pleaded with Ch'ao not to endanger himself on this expedition also. In Chin's version of the story, Sung's pleadings are all put into the mouth of Wu Yung, and Sung remains silent most of the time.

6. Whiting the background (*pei-mien p'u-fen fa*).[68] Mr. Irwin paraphrases this technique as "emphasis through contrast." And Chin himself explains it thus: "For example, in order to bring out Sung Chiang's deceitfulness (*chien-cha*), the author inevitably writes about Li K'uei's straightforwardness (*chen-shuai*)." [69]

As Irwin notes, one of the most artistic aspects of the *Shui-hu chuan* is the handling of the relationship between Sung Chiang and Li K'uei: "From the time of their first meeting they are attracted to each other by their disparity in temperament, and the development of their relationship throughout the course of the novel is a manifestation of psychological insight deserving the highest praise." [70] Professor C. T. Hsia in *The Classic Chinese Novel* calls attention to the same fact and discusses it at some length: "Li K'uei is the prime symbol of that dark force, just as his master and friend Sung Chiang is the prime symbol of Confucian service to the throne. In the subtle interactions of this inseparable pair exist the ideological tensions of the novel." At the same time, as Professor Hsia goes on to say in the next paragraph, "the complementary characters of Sung Chiang and Li K'uei provide whatever thematic unity the novel achieves despite its contentment with an episodic and mechanically plotted narrative." [71] Without endorsing his prejudiced attitude toward Sung Chiang, we must therefore give credit to Chin for being probably the first critic to have pointed out this stylistic device in the novel.

7. Laying out the bait (*nung-yin fa*). Chin's own explanation of this technique is clear enough: "This means that the author has something important to write about; but he cannot very well start abruptly, so he first makes up a passage of minor interest to lead into it."

8. The tail of an otter (*t'a-wei fa*). That this technique is meant to be complementary to the previous one can be seen in the following explanation by Chin: "After the account of an exciting event, the author cannot very well bring his story to a sudden

stop, so he further makes up a few short passages in order to bring it to a gradual end." If we may call "laying out the bait" the prologue to a major action, then this technique can be considered the epilogue to the same.

9. Open breach of the law (*cheng-fan fa*). What Chin means by this term is that Shih Nai-an sometimes purposely chose similar topics to write about, and yet had the skill not to repeat himself. Three times in the novel, for example, Shih writes about tiger fights, but each description differs sufficiently from the others.[72] This, in Chin's mind, demonstrates Shih's resourcefulness as a writer.

10. Minor breach of the law (*lüeh-fan fa*). This technique is but a variation of the preceding. Shih Nai-an sometimes constructed situations which, though not so similar as the preceding examples, still bear some resemblance to each other.

11. Extreme lavishness (*chi-pu-sheng fa*). "For example, in order to make Sung Chiang offend against the law, the author wrote about the gold in his portfolio (*chao-wen-tai*); and before this, Yen P'o-hsi's *amour* with Chang San; and before this, Sung Chiang's marriage with Yen P'o-hsi; and before this, Sung Chiang's donation of a coffin to the Yen family (Chapts. 19–20). But all these passages are peripheral to the main story." That is to say, the main story here is Sung Chiang's violation of the law by killing his unfaithful wife. All the other stories mentioned here are mere incidents leading to it. In this case the author is lavish with peripheral incidents.

12. Extreme frugality (*chi-sheng fa*). This is of course the opposite of the preceding technique. Here the author adopts a device that will enable him to avoid repetition without loss to the narrative.

13. Releasing a thing with a view to recapturing it (*yü ho ku tsung fa*). We would call this suspense. The first example given by Chin refers to the rescue of Sung Chiang from the execution ground at Chiang-chou (Chapter 39). After Sung and the rescue team fight their way out to a temple by the side of a river, they are met by three boats manned by Li Chün, the Chang and T'ung brothers. At that juncture, however, Li K'uei wants to return to the city to kill the Magistrate, thus creating a further delay in the rescue and suspense in the reader. The second example is also connected with Sung Chiang. In his mission to take his father and

the whole family to Liang-shan-p'o, Sung is trapped one night in a temple to the Goddess of the Ninth Heaven (Chapter 41). Had it not been for the divine protection of the Goddess, he would certainly have been captured. Everytime Chao Neng and Chao Te, the leaders of the pursuing band, come near Sung's hiding place, a strong gust of wind arises, blowing out their torches and filling their eyes with dust. Startled by such a supernatural wind, they retreat from the temple. Just as they are stepping out of the gate of the temple, however, they hear the screams of a soldier who in a state of fright has tripped on the end of a tree. This small incident renders the atmosphere even more tense and frightening.

14. Clouds cutting the mountain in halves (*heng-yun tuan shan fa*). "For example, after the second attack on the Chu Family Village [and before the third attack], suddenly comes the story of Hsieh Chen and Hsieh Pao's quarrel [with old lord Mao] over the carcass of a tiger, and their subsequent escape from jail (Chapter 48). . . . This is because when an episode is too long, it may seem tiresome. The author therefore interrupts it in the middle (*i.e.* digresses), so as to separate it into two parts." Thus this technique, derived from painting, bears some resemblance to the device of comic relief in a serious tragedy.

15. Joining a broken zither string with glue (*luan-chiao hsü hsien fa*). The example given here by Chin takes place in Chapter 61. Yang Hsiung and Shih Hsiu are sent down Liang-shan-p'o to find out more about Lu Chün-yi's situation at Ta-ming Fu. On the other hand, Yen Ch'ing, Lu Chün-yi's servant, is on his way to Liang-shan-p'o to report Lu's arrest and also to seek help. Both parties take short cuts to save time. On the way, Yen Ch'ing shoots a magpie with an arrow to foretell the success of his mission. The wounded magpie leads Yen Ch'ing on until he meets with Yang Hsiung and Shih Hsiu on another small road. Yen Ch'ing has never been to Liang-shan-p'o, so the two parties are unknown to each other. In the scuffle which follows, Yen Ch'ing fells Shih Hsiu with his fist, only to be subdued by Yang Hsiung. Yen Ch'ing reveals his name and his mission, and the two parties are reconciled and go about their business. What Chin wants to say here is that in order to bring the two unknown parties together, Shih Nai-an, as a conscientious artist, carefully lays out a string of incidents which make the rendezvous seem plausible.

To the modern reader, some of the fifteen techniques noted

above will no doubt appear mechanical, and indeed superficial. On the other hand, the fact that some of them are readily trans-latable into modern critical terms such as "satire," "contrast," "sus-pense," etc. bespeaks the modernity of Chin's critical thinking. Taken as a whole, and given the proper historical perspective, they serve as a fair index to his insight and perceptiveness as a critic.

V   The Highly Individual Style of the Commentary

Chin's *Shui-hu* commentary would be very dull reading indeed if it consisted only of laying out the fifteen techniques. The truth of the matter is that in the main body of the commentary, espe-cially in the scattered remarks interspersed in the text, Chin wrote with a refreshingly original and highly individual style, which has since appealed greatly to scholars and writers alike who advocate the cultivation and expression of personal taste.[73] In fact, many passages can be lifted from the commentary and read as short independent essays, strongly suggestive of the "familiar essays" written in England during the Romantic period and afterwards. As is the case with the familiar essay, when we read such passages in Chin's commentary, we feel as though we are chatting with an old and intimate friend with whom we may not always agree, but whose little prejudices and eccentricities we can appreciate and enjoy.

Like any informal chat, Chin's running comments are character-ized by a certain discursive and rambling quality sometimes mis-taken for confusion and disorderliness. Tung Han (*fl.* 1659), for one, felt so and aired his strong disapproval in the following man-ner: "In the district of Wu there was a man by the name of Chin Sheng-t'an who had written [commentaries on] the works of gen-ius. . . . His remarks were wild and unorthodox, and funny ex-pressions and vulgar sentences filled his pages. . . . Take the book *Hsi-hsiang* for example. . . . In one instance he would speak in the Wu dialect, and in another he would quote from the classics: it is disorderly and improper."[74] And yet to us, Chin's seemingly unscrupulous use of the language is exactly what makes him such an interesting writer. In reading him, we are not merely going over some dry and contrived treatises. Instead, we are watching the gradual unfolding of a very interesting and highly original mind. Moreover, the "disorderliness" as noted by Tung Han is only superficial. Underneath it, as any careful and unbiased reader can perceive, are coherent and intelligent discussions of whatever happens to be the topic on hand. Perhaps the best way to illustrate this aspect of his style (and for that matter his general critical acumen) is to translate with Chin's comments the episode of Wu Sung's fight with the tiger in Chapter 22, to which several references have been made.

On his way to visit his brother in another part of the country, Wu Sung comes one afternoon to a wine-shop a few miles from a mountain ridge which later he has to cross on his journey. After consuming altogether eighteen bowls of wine, he is in no mood to heed the innkeeper's warning not to cross the ridge alone on account of the presence of a tiger on the mountain, so he sets out on his journey again. In the following translation, Chin's remarks are italicized and put in brackets. It should also be pointed out that the main narrative in the episode agrees well with the older edition. The frequency of the mention of the word "club," which Chin emphasizes in his comments, is exactly the same in the two versions.[75]

Wu Sung carried his club [*Club the ninth time. Carried his club— the third posture he assumes with the club*],[76] and in big strides went toward the Ching-yang Ridge in spite of the innkeeper's warning. After having gone about four or five *li*, he came to the foot of the ridge. There he saw a huge tree, the bark of which had been scraped away, so that there was a patch of white wood. On the white patch were written two columns of characters. Wu Sung could recognize quite a few characters, so when he raised his head to look, he saw written: "Because of the great tiger on the Ching-yang Ridge, that has been inflicting harm on the people recently, if there are travelers passing, they should pass in groups and between the hours from mid-morning to mid-afternoon. Please do not endanger yourselves." [*Extraordinary writing (ch'i-wen).*]

After having read the instruction, Wu Sung laughed and said, "This is a trick played by the innkeeper to frighten the travelers, so that they will stay in his inn. What damned thing should I be afraid of?" Holding his club sideways [*Club: the tenth time. Holding his club sideways— the fourth posture he assumes with the club*], he walked up the ridge.

At that time it was already late in the afternoon, and the red sun, like a wheel, was slowly rolling down the side of the mountain. [*Frightening scenery.*]

Wu Sung walked up the ridge heedlessly on the strength of the wine.

In less than half a *li*, he came upon an abandoned shrine to a mountain spirit. [*Extraordinary writing. Were it not for this shrine, there would be almost no place for pasting the proclamation.*] Approaching the front of the shrine, he saw pasted on the door a proclamation with an official seal. When Wu Sung stopped to read, he saw there written: "A Proclamation from the District of Yang-ku: On Ching-yang Ridge, recently a big tiger has taken the lives of people. At present, the heads of various villages as well as hunters have been given a deadline for capturing the tiger on pain of flogging. They have not yet succeeded. For this reason, if there are passing travelers, they are instructed to cross the ridge in groups and during the hours from mid-morning to mid-afternoon. No one is allowed to cross the ridge by himself, or at other times, lest he lose his life. Everyone should take note of this. Proclaimed on such a day in such a month of such a year in the reign period Cheng-ho." [*Extraordinary writing.*]

After finishing the proclamation, Wu Sung began to realize that truly there was a tiger. He was about to turn about to go back to the wine shop [*With this sign of weakness, Wu Sung's valor is brought out even more clearly. Otherwise, it would mean that things happened too suddenly, and Wu Sung simply could not avoid meeting the tiger, and that he was lucky to have escaped from the mouth of the tiger*],[77] when he thought to himself, "If I go back, I shall be ridiculed by him (*i.e.* the innkeeper) for not being a brave man. I will not turn back." [*Isn't it unusual (yi) to stake one's life for the sake of fame?*] After debating with himself for a while, he said, "What damned thing am I afraid of? Let me just go up and see what will happen." [*Wu Sung's valor is vividly portrayed.*]

As Wu Sung walked, the fumes of the wine rose up in his head. [*See how methodically the author writes about drunkenness!*] So he whisked away his felt-hat to hang on his back [*This is winter time, but the author insists on describing the great heat felt by Wu Sung. Later when the big tiger jumps at him, he is so scared as to shed cold sweat. A superb writer!*], tucked the club underneath his arm [*Club: the eleventh time. Tucked the club underneath his arm—the fifth posture he assumes with the club*], and step by step went up the ridge. He turned his head around to look at the sun, and saw that it was gradually going down. [*Frightening scenery. If I were there at that time, even if there were no tiger coming out, I would cry aloud.*] This was right in the midst of the tenth month. The days were short and the nights long, and it grew dark very quickly. [*This is the author's own explanatory note.*] Wu Sung mumbled to himself, "What big tiger is there? People just scare themselves and dare not climb the hill." [*Again the author lets Wu Sung comfort himself.*] After Wu Sung had walked for a while, the strength of the wine became apparent. [*Drunk.*] He began to feel scorchingly hot inside. [*Hot.*] With one hand carrying the club [*Club: the twelfth time. Again he carries the club—the sixth posture he assumes with the club*] and the other opening up his coat at the chest [*A superb picture*], he stumbled and staggered, and blundered straight through a forest of tangled trees. [*Frightening scenery. We know it is a forest for tigers.*] He saw a high, smooth, bluish rock. [*After having made Wu Sung pass the tangled trees, the author might be expected to let the tiger jump out. Instead, he conjures up a piece of blue rock, and almost lets Wu Sung fall asleep on it. After having caused the reader to be worried to death, he then brings out the tiger. How incorrigible (k'o hen, but used good-naturedly) is the man of genius!*] He leaned his club against the side of the rock [*The club was leaned to the side—the seventh posture Wu Sung assumes with the club. Club: the thirteenth time*] and was just about to lay himself down upon the rock to sleep [*The reader is frightened to death*], when there rose a violent gust of wind. After the gust of wind had passed, Wu Sung heard a great crash behind the tangled trees, and out leaped a big tiger with slanting eyes and white forehead. [*The tiger came out with force and power.*] Seeing it, Wu Sung cried "Ah-ya!" and rolled down from the blue rock. [*With this sign of weakness, Wu Sung's valor is brought out even more clearly. Otherwise, it would be like the story of Tzu-lu*[78] *told in a small village, extremely untrue to life.*] Grasping the club in his hand [*Club: the fourteenth time. Grasping the club—the eighth posture he assumes with the club*], he dodged to the side of the blue rock. [*The first dodging. From here on the man becomes a superman and the tiger a live tiger. The reader must pay very close attention from paragraph to paragraph. I have often thought that there are places to see a painted tiger, but none to see a genuine one; one can see a genuine tiger that is dead, but not one that is living; a living tiger walking can probably be seen occasionally, but a living tiger battling with a man—there are never places to see such a thing. Now suddenly in an almost casual way Nai-an with his pen has painted a complete picture of a living tiger battling with a man. From now on those who want to see a tiger can all come to the Ching-yang Ridge in the Shui-hu chuan to stare to their satisfaction. Moreover, they need not be frightened. What a great kindness Nai-an has rendered to his readers! It is said that Chao Sung-hsüeh*[79] *was fond of painting horses. In his latter years, his technique became even more penetrating. Whenever he wished to meditate on how to paint a new picture, he would loosen his clothes in a secluded room and crouch on the floor. He would learn first how to be a horse, and then order a brush. One day Lady Kuan*[80] *came upon him in this process, and Chao even appeared to be a horse. Now when Nai-an was writing this passage, could it be that he too had loosened his clothes, and while crouching on the ground, assumed the postures of a pounce,*]

a kick, and a cut (by the tiger)? [81] *Su Tung-p'o in a poem on a painting of geese wrote:*

> *When wild geese see the approach of a man,*
> *They appear startled even before taking off.*
> *From what hidden place have you observed them,*
> *To catch this natural pose of theirs so oblivious*
> *of man?*

*I really don't know where in his mind Nai-an obtained this method of
painting a tiger eating a man. When I say that of all writers of the past
three thousand years he alone is a genius, is this mere empty praise?*]

   The big tiger was both hungry and thirsty. With just a light touch
on the ground with its two front paws, it gathered itself and sprang
through the air. [*The tiger.*] Wu Sung was frightened and the wine in
him came out in a cold sweat. [*Subtle and marvelous writing (shen-
miao chih pi). As I was reading this under the lamp, the light seemed
to shrink into the shape of a bean, and its color became green.*] [82] In
less time than it takes to tell it, when Wu Sung saw that the tiger was
coming down upon him, with one quick move he dodged behind it.
[*The man. The second dodging.*] Now it is most difficult for a tiger
to see someone behind its back. [*In the midst of this turmoil the author
takes time out to provide an explanatory note.*] It therefore dug its
front paws into the ground, and with one sweep lifted up its back and
rear parts to kick. [*The tiger.*] With a single quick move Wu Sung
dodged to one side. [*The man. The third dodging.*] Seeing that it could
not kick Wu Sung, the tiger let out a tremendous roar which, like a
thunderclap in the sky, shook the whole mountain ridge. It then erected
its tail like an iron staff, and slashed down. [*The tiger.*] But Wu Sung
again dodged to one side. [*The man. The fourth dodging.*] Ordinarily
when a tiger tries to seize a man, it does so only with a pounce, a kick,
and a cut. If after these three maneuvers it can not seize a man, half
of its heart and temper desert it. [*In the midst of this turmoil the author
takes time out to provide an explanatory note. A genius, commanding
a wide acquaintance with things, certainly does not speak falsely. However, there is no place to verify this statement of his. This passage
brings all the previous action to an end. In what has gone above, Wu
Sung only used the method of dodging four times. In what follows he
will apply his strength.*]

   Unable to cut Wu Sung with its tail, the tiger roared again, and
swiftly circled round. [*The tiger.*] Seeing that the tiger had again
turned, Wu Sung raised his club with both hands [*Raised his club—
the ninth posture he assumes with the club. Club: the fifteenth time*]

and with all his strength brought it down from mid-air in one swift blow. [*The man. After this blow, who would not think that the tiger will be done away with? And yet unexpected things are going to take place.*] There was a crashing sound, and leaves and branches scattered down over his face. When he fixed his eyes to see, Wu Sung found that he had not hit the tiger [*He had marshaled all his strength and yet he did not hit the tiger. What a hair-raising sentence!*], instead in his haste he had hit a withered tree. [*In this turmoil the author again takes time out to provide this explanatory note.*]The club broke in two, and he was only holding half of it in his hand. [*Club: the sixteenth time. The author has been busy writing about the club for a long while. We all thought that Wu Sung could rely on it to strike the tiger, but all of a sudden it comes to nought here: we are absolutely stunned and hardly dare read on. After the club is broken, Wu Sung's extraordinary power of fighting the tiger with his bare hands can be revealed. However, the reader is so frightened that his heart and liver have jumped out of his mouth.*]

The tiger roared, its wrath fully aroused. Turning its body around, it again leaped toward Wu Sung. [*The tiger.*] Wu Sung again jumped away and retreated ten steps. [*The man.*] No sooner had he done so, than the tiger planted its two forepaws right in front of him. [*The tiger.*] Seizing the opportunity, Wu Sung threw away the broken club [*The club is got rid of. Club: the seventeenth time*], and with the same motion both his hands clutched the tiger's spotted neck, and pressed the head down. [*The man.*] The tiger in desperation attempted to struggle loose [*The tiger*], but Wu Sung forced it down with all his strength, unwilling to relax his grip even for a moment. [*The man.*] Then he kicked the tiger's face and eyes wildly. [*Kicking with a foot— marvelous. For he cannot loosen his hands. Kicking the eyes—marvelous. For it would be hard to kick any other spot.*] The tiger began to roar, and clawed up two heaps of yellow mud underneath its body, forming a mud pit. [*The tiger. How did Nai-an know that the man who kicks at a tiger must kick its eyes, and that when a tiger is being kicked at, it will make a mud pit? All this is improbable writing, and yet the matter must be a certainty. How absolutely extraordinary! How absolutely marvelous!*][83] Wu Sung pressed the tiger's mouth straight into the pit. [*The man.*] Being so mauled by Wu Sung, the tiger became completely worn out. [*The tiger.*]

Wu Sung then used his left hand to grasp tightly the tiger's spotted neck, and freeing the right hand, lifted up his hammerlike fist and bludgeoned the tiger with all his strength. [*The man.*] After fifty or seventy blows, blood began to gush out from the tiger's eyes, mouth, nose, and ears. The tiger, unable to stir any more, could barely gasp for breath. [*The tiger.*] Wu Sung let go of the beast, and went among the pine trees in search of his broken club. Grasping the broken club in his hand, and fearing lest the tiger was not yet dead, he struck it again. [*Club: the eighteenth time. This is the last sound of the club.*] Only after he saw the tiger's breathing cease did he finally throw down the club. [*The club ends here.*] He then thought to himself, "I'll just pick up the tiger and drag it down the ridge." [*His first thought is to take it way. Marvelous.*] But when he tried to pull the tiger from its pool of blood with his both hands, he couldn't! The truth was he had completely used up his strength, and all his limbs were weak and powerless. [*With this sign of weakness his powers of a moment ago become even more evident.*]

Wu Sung returned to the blue rock and sat there for a while. [*Wu Sung's extreme weariness depicted here brings out more clearly through contrast his great prowess of a moment ago. The narrative comes back to the blue rock again. Absolutely marvelous!*] He thought to himself, "It is getting dark. Suppose another tiger leaps out, how will I subdue it? I'd better get down the ridge somehow, and come back tomorrow morning to take care of the beast." [*The sentence is specially designed so as to make what follows appear surprising.*] [84] He then found his felt-hat by the side of the rock [*With a cry "Ah-yah!" he rolled down from the blue rock. At that moment he was so frightened out of his wits that he hadn't noticed where his hat had dropped. Penetrating writing*], went through the tangled trees [*The author comes back to the tangled trees*], and dragged himself down the ridge a step at a time.

This episode is considered a classic of Chinese fiction. Its vivid language and its detailed and orderly account of the struggle between man and beast are high points in the development of Chinese fiction. Chin was equal to his task when he undertook to criticize this well-known passage. He makes two perceptive and revealing points. Although Wu Sung is a brave man, he is in no sense a superman. His hesitations over going on after learning about the existence of the tiger and his momentary loss of heart upon seeing the tiger itself only make his later performance seem the more courageous and true to life. This is an important point because had Wu Sung been treated as a superman here, we would have lost a great deal of our interest in him because the outcome of the fight would never have been in doubt. Chin also brings home the significance of the club in the episode. We watch Wu Sung carrying his club, his sole means of defense, and then when the critical moment comes, it breaks. The reader feels almost as bereft as Wu Sung. This is, of course, a trick played by the author, but it is a clever and highly effective one, and we feel a sense of gratitude to Chin for pointing it out.

The Western reader may resent being constantly interrupted by somebody else's comments while reading the story, and that the overabundant use of such general, vague expressions as "Extraordinary writing" and "How marvelous!" is irritating. Nevertheless, if we just take Chin's remarks by themselves, or better yet, if after we have read through the narrative once, we then come back to read Chin's comments, we can hardly fail to be affected by his infectious enthusiasm. We are disarmed to hear that had he been traveling in such deserted and gloomy surroundings, even if there were no tiger around, he would have cried out in fear. As the tension mounts in the story, so does Chin's until we are told how the very light from the lamp seems to shrink and take on a greenish cast while he reads this episode. The story of Chao Sung-hsüeh and his horses, while digressive in nature, is also quite illuminating from a critical point of view. It vividly illustrates (by analogy) Shih Nai-an's extraordinary success in the portrayal of the tiger. In short, as we go over Chin's scattered remarks, we can always sense behind them the presence of a lively, genuinely affected, and sensitive individual who is uninhibited in expressing what he felt when reading this passage. Some people today read Chin's commentary not only because it contains many critical insights but also because it is written in such a delightfully personal style. The celebrated essayist Chou Tso-jen's (1885–1967) comment in his *Chiu-shu hui-hsiang chi* (*Recalling Old Books*) in this regard is illustrative: "Of all commentaries on fiction, Chin Sheng-t'an's are of course the best. . . . When I read the *Shui-hu chuan,* I pay equal attention to the main text and to the comments. It is like eating white fungus (*pai mu-erh,* a Chinese delicacy); they taste even better eaten with soup." [85]

CHAPTER 5

The Hsi-hsiang *Commentary*

I *The Story and Its Historical Development*

*H*SI-HSIANG CHI or *The Romance of the Western Chamber* is a thirteenth-century Yuan dynasty play of twenty-one acts in five parts. Authored by Wang Te-hsin (better known by his *tzu* Shih-fu), it is celebrated for its daring description of a secret love affair between a young scholar (Chang Sheng) and the daughter of a Chief Minister of the T'ang period (Ts'ui Ying-ying). According to the play, Chang meets Ying-ying in a Buddhist monastery where she and her mother have stopped while escorting the coffin of her father, who had recently died, to their native town. Chang falls in love with her immediately. But since Ying-ying is constantly watched by her mother, he can only express his love for her by reciting a poem behind the wall of the courtyard in which they have taken lodging. Shortly afterwards, however, an unexpected event takes place, which finally brings Chang and Ying-ying together. The word of Ying-ying's extraordinary beauty reaches the ear of a bandit, Sun the Flying Tiger, who, determined to have her as a consort, dispatches a band of ruffians to surround the monastery. Because of the emergency, Ying-ying's mother agrees that whoever drives the bandits away can have Ying-ying as his wife. It happens that Chang Sheng's childhood friend, General Tu, is stationed not far from the monastery, and Chang immediately sends him a letter asking for help. Upon the arrival of General Tu and his troops, Sun the Flying Tiger is subdued, and the bandits dispersed. Chang Sheng and Ying-ying are now filled with anticipation of their promised marriage. But their happiness proves to be premature. Madame Ts'ui, Ying-ying's mother, begins to regret her rash decision and takes back her word with the excuse that Ying-ying has already been betrothed to the son of another high official of the court. Both Chang Sheng and Ying-

ying are greatly disappointed and begin to pine away with their unfulfilled love. Fortunately, Ying-ying's capable and intelligent maid, Hung Niang, takes pity on them, and through a series of ingenious arrangements finally succeeds in bringing them together in a secret union. Later the fact is found out by Madame Ts'ui, who, in order to cover up the "shame," reluctantly consents to Ying-ying's marrying Chang on one condition: Chang must leave for the capital to take part in the civil service examinations. The marriage will depend entirely upon his success or failure. Heartbroken, Chang and Ying-ying bid farewell to each other. Chang, however, proves to be not only a faithful lover but also a brilliant scholar. He passes the examinations with highest honors and is appointed to high office. They are thus able to marry each other in the end.

The story, outlined above, represents the culmination of a long historical development. The romance between Chang Sheng and Ts'ui Ying-ying was first told in a T'ang *ch'uan-ch'i* (short story in literary Chinese) by Yuan Chen (770–831), called *The Story of Ying-ying* (*Ying-ying chuan*), sometimes also known as *The Story of Meeting a Fairy* (*Hui chen chi*).[1] As in the play, in the short story Chang meets Ying-ying in a Buddhist monastery, and is immediately struck with lovesickness. Again, as in the play, Chang finally succeeds in fulfilling his wishes by secretly living together with Ying-ying for a time. But unlike the Chang in the play—and here is the most important difference between the two—the Chang of the short story for some reason ultimately breaks with Ying-ying and does not ask for her hand in marriage. In spite of (or because of?) such an unhappy ending, the account of the secret love between the young scholar and the girl had a strong appeal to later writers and storytellers. A huge corpus of recitative literature began to grow up around the original story.[2] At the same time, however, probably under the pressures of popular demand, storytellers began to modify the story, so that the hero and the heroine were happily married to each other in the end. The first example of the modified version of the story we have is a medley (*chu-kung-tiao*)[3]—a type of oral performance by one man, alternating in prose and verse and with instrumental accompaniment—known variously as *Hsien-so Hsi-hsiang*, *Hsi-hsiang ch'ou-t'an-tz'u*, and *Hsi-hsiang chi chu-kung-tiao* by a certain Tung Chieh-yuan of the Chin dynasty (1115–1234). The *Hsi-*

hsiang chi, with which we are concerned and whose story has been outlined above, was closely modeled upon Tung's medley.[4]

II *Is* Hsi-hsiang *Immoral?*

The editing and annotating of the *Hsi-hsiang chi* represents Chin's first major critical effort after the fall of the Ming in 1644. One immediate problem he had to face was to decide whether the book is immoral or not. Since, as we have seen in the outline of the story above, Ying-ying and Chang Sheng fulfilled their love outside the marriage bond, and since the scene of their first secret union is described in language that is unambiguous, even though symbolic, the *Hsi-hsiang chi* was traditionally considered by the moralists as an indecent, immoral, and licentious work, whose place was high on the list of forbidden books. T'ang Lai-ho (*chin-shih* of 1640) is thus reported to have said, "I heard that in the 1590s the performance of the *Hsi-hsiang chi* . . . was still forbidden among [good] families." [5] Kuei Chuang (1613–1673), great-grandson of Kuei Yu-kuang (1506–1571) and a contemporary of Chin, bluntly called the play "a book teaching debauchery." [6]

Chin's reaction to the strait-laced moralists was a mixture of impatience and amusement. "*Hsi-hsiang chi* is definitely not an indecent book. . . ," [7] he declares, and those who say that *Hsi-hsiang chi* is indecent "will certainly fall into the hell where tongues are uprooted." [8] Another punishment proper for these people would be a good flogging: "If someone says the *Hsi-hsiang chi* is a licentious book, all he needs is a good flogging. There is no need to lecture him. Why is this so? Because he only heard this in his youth from a village schoolmaster. But once he heard it, he committed it to his mind. In reality he has never set his eyes on *Hsi-hsiang chi.* Truly even to flog him is to do him wrong [since he does not know what he is talking about]!" [9]

But why should people call *Hsi-hsiang chi* immoral? The reason, as Chin saw it, is actually very simple. ". . . It is only because there is this thing (*i.e.* sex) in it." [10] This is wrong, of course, as Chin goes on to argue: "If we consider 'this thing' more carefully, what day is without it? What place is without it? Can we say that because there is 'this thing' between Heaven and Earth, therefore Heaven and Earth should be abolished? If we think carefully whence this body of ours comes, can we say this body of ours should therefore be discarded?" [11] In the Introductory Remarks to Act I of Part IV, where the lovers meet in their first rendezvous, the same argument is used and a distinction between literature and mere licentious writing is made:

> Some people say this is the most obscene part of the *Hsi-hsiang chi*. This is indeed the opinion of a narrow-minded schoolmaster of a small hamlet. For if we talk about "this thing," then since the time of the legendary P'an Ku down to the present day, which household has not had it? But if we talk about this writing, then also since the time of P'an Ku down to the present day, from whose pen has there been such fine writing? If there is no household which does not have "this thing," what obscenity is there about it? If from no other man's pen can there be such fine writing, who dare say there is one phrase or even one word which is obscene in it? . . . The "thing" is what can be found in every household, whereas the writing is that of one man. The reason why the author makes a pretext of something found in every household to write what is of his own concern is because his mind is on writing not on the "thing." Since his mind is not on the "thing," therefore he will not shun what is obscene. Since his mind is rather on writing, therefore he truly hasn't seen anything obscene. But those narrow-minded small village schoolmasters are still making a ceaseless hubbub, condemning the writing as obscene. Isn't this due to the fact that the schoolmasters not only don't understand the writing, but on the other hand are only too understanding of "this thing?" This being the case, of all the obscene people in the world, none can surpass those schoolmasters. How dare they make a ceaseless hubbub? [12]

What Chin seems to say here is that we must draw a line between what is genuine literature and what is mere obscenity. The difference here is one of intention. A literary masterpiece may contain elements of sex, but as long as the author's intention is not sex, or in other words, as long as the purpose of the work is not just sex, it cannot be considered an obscene book.[13] If people insist that such a masterpiece is immoral, the fault lies not with the book, but rather with the people who are themselves lascivious-minded.

Perhaps Chin's most weighty argument for the dignity of *Hsi-hsiang chi* is the similarity he saw between it and the *Book of Poetry*, a Confucian canon which contains many daring, outspoken love lyrics. If the *Book of Poetry*, in spite of its love lyrics, can pass as a classic, Chin argues, why not the *Hsi-hsiang chi?*

"When young scholars want to read the *Hsi-hsiang chi,* let them first read the folk songs in the *Shih-ching (Book of Poetry).* What is being described in the *Hsi-hsiang chi* is exactly what is being described in the folk songs of the *Shih-ching*." [14] This being the case, the *Hsi-hsiang chi* must no longer be brushed aside as something improper or trivial. It is not only not improper or trivial, Chin further contends, but on the contrary, it contains the most excellent writing in the world.[15] Before we can examine the details of Chin's praise of the play's artistic achievement, however, we must first look at his editorial procedure and the changes he made in the text.

III   *His Editorial Procedure and Emendations of the Text*

The editorial procedure Chin followed in the *Hsi-hsiang chi* is the same as in the *Shui-hu chuan.* Two prefaces stating his purpose in undertaking such a project are followed by eighty-one notes on how to read the play. Each act in the play is, as a rule, preceded by a section of Introductory Remarks discussing in general terms the theme or artistic achievement of the act concerned. The act is then broken up into many small sections, each followed by a brief explanation of what is being described or stated in the section. Within the section, critical remarks are liberally planted here and there, between lines, phrases, and even words.

As in the case of the *Shui-hu chuan,* Chin's work as a critic is not confined to providing critical remarks. Whenever he deemed it desirable, he did not hesitate to make textual changes in the play. Many of his deletions and changes seem to have stemmed from his desire to make Chang Sheng and Ying-ying act and speak according to their social background. (Both are talented and well-educated young people from prominent families.) More often, however, he tampered with the text for the sole purpose of achieving superior literary effects. Since we shall have occasion to see some examples of the first category in (IV B) below,[16] let us concentrate here on examples of the second kind. Moreover, since the play consists alternately of sung lyrics and spoken parts (in prose), this part of Chin's critical effort can be conveniently examined in two sections.

A *Changes Made in the Lyrics*

The lyrics in the play were written to musical airs drawn from an existing repertoire. The metrical restrictions were stringent (the tone of each syllable was prescribed, for instance, and rhyme was required) and this fact prevented Chin from making any large-scale alteration in the lyrics. His most common practice was to shorten or eliminate entirely the so-called "padding words" (*ch'en-tzu*)—supernumerary words, the addition or deletion of which does not affect the basic metrical patterns. As for the words that do count in the metrical pattern, he changed only one or two here and there. Even so, however, he sometimes made changes in violation of the rules of prosody. For example, one of a series of songs sung by Chang Sheng on his first appearance in the play (Part I, Act I) is written to the air "Yu hu-lu" (The Oily Bottle Gourd). The very first line in this song reads as follows in an older edition of the play:[17] "Chiu ch'ü feng t'ao ho ch'u hsien— Where along the nine-curved [river] (*i.e.* the Yellow River) are the winds and waves more prominent?"[18] In Chin's version, however, the line reads slightly differently: "Chiu ch'ü feng t'ao ho ch'u hsien—Where along the nine-curved [river] are the winds and waves more treacherous?"[19] That is to say, the last character (a rhyme word) in the line "hsien" (prominent) is changed into "hsien" (treacherous). These two characters, which rhyme in modern Mandarin and apparently also rhymed in Chin's own dialect (Wu), unfortunately did not rhyme during Yuan times, the former ending in -n and the latter in -m.[20] The former, according to the rhyme book *Chung-yuan yin-yun* (*The Phonology of the Dialect of North China*), belongs to the "hsien t'ien" rhyme category, while the latter that of "lien hsien."[21] Thus Chin may have gained some literary effectiveness by using the word "treacherous" rather than "prominent," but he had unwittingly transgressed against the rhyming prescription.

Another example of a slightly different type occurs in Part III, Act I. In the song sung by Hung Niang to the air "Ch'ing ko-erh" (The Little Blue Brother?), the penultimate line should consist of seven characters, with the last one a rhyme word.[22] This is indeed the case in the older edition: "[Tse shuo tao] tso yeh t'an ch'in [ti] na jen erh—[I will then say that] the one [who] played the lute last night."[23] Disregarding the "padding words" placed in brackets, there are exactly seven characters in the line, and the last character "erh" rhymes. In Chin's version, however, this line is changed to: "[Wo chih shuo] tso yeh t'an ch'in na jen—[I will just say that] the one playing the lute last night." [24] What Chin did, then, was to rephrase the first three "padding words," "Tse shuo tao" (I will then say), as "Wo chih shuo" (I will just say that), while simply cutting out the remaining "padding word," "ti" (who) in the line. So far, so good. But when he then proceeded to excise the last character "erh" in the line, he violated the metrical rules. Although the character "erh," being a nominal suffix, does not add much to the total meaning of the line, it nevertheless is needed to complete the rhyme, as well as to make up the required number of characters in the line. Hence Chin's version may appear neater and more economical from a literary point of view, but it is metrically incorrect.

The above two examples should be sufficient to illustrate the kinds of risks Chin ran when he undertook to tamper with the sung passages in the play.

B *Changes Made in the Spoken Parts*

In the case of the spoken parts, being unrestricted by any formal requirements, Chin was much more free with his material. For example, in Act I of Part I, after Chang sees Ying-ying in the courtyard of the monastery, he is so struck by her dazzling beauty that in the hope of living near her he asks Fa Ts'ung, the Superior's disciple who is accompanying him, to arrange for him to live in the monastery. Here is the request (in the older edition): "May I trouble you to say to your Superior: if he has unoccupied rooms, I should like to rent a corner so as to study the classics and histories morning and evening. It would be better than living in a noisy, disorderly inn. I will gladly pay whatever is customary. I should like to move in tomorrow." [25] Chang Sheng comes the next day (Part I, Act II), and the very first song he sings to himself begins with the following two lines: "If you don't help me [secure a room],/I will blame you forever Monk Fa Ts'ung!" [26] He has not seen Fa Ts'ung yet, nor does he know what will happen to his request, and yet he is already anticipating a possible setback. The nervousness and anxiety of Chang Sheng, created by the extreme importance he attaches to his mission, are vividly revealed. However, in the hope of bringing out Chang's anxiety even more viv-

idly, Chin did two things in his version of the play: First, he
deleted the request Chang made to Fa Ts'ung about renting a
room at the end of Act I, thereby making Chang's pronounce-
ment, "If you don't help me . . ." in the beginning of Act II
sound very sudden, abrupt, and indeed puzzling. Second, he
added two sentences spoken by Fa Ts'ung right after the pro-
nouncement to make what was originally a soliloquy into a speech
addressed directly to Fa Ts'ung, who now appears utterly puzzled:
"You have come, Sir. I don't know what you are talking about." [27]
Chin's primary purpose in making such changes is therefore to
stress the agitated state of mind Chang is in at the moment: he
has decided that the best way to see Ying-ying again would be to
live near her by renting a room in the monastery. Yet he cannot be
sure he will be allowed to do so. If he cannot rent a room, his
whole hope, and at that moment his whole dream in life, will be
crushed. The more he turns this thought over in his head, the
more nervous and restless he becomes, until he is so distracted
that when he does see Fa Ts'ung again, he bluntly thrusts his ap-
prehensive feelings on the latter without remembering that he has
not made his request for help yet. For fear the reader may fail to
grasp the subtlety and significance of his revision, Chin provided
in his Introductory Remarks to the act a long paragraph stating
just that. He concluded admiringly, "Thus at one stroke of the pen
within the first two lines, in just thirteen characters, the author has
most thoroughly and vividly described the plight of Chang Sheng
after a sleepless night." [28]

Textual changes in Chin's edition such as this are innumerable.
The net result is that from a purely literary viewpoint Chin's version reads better than the older one. But on the other hand, we
must not forget that in a sung poetic play such as the *Hsi-hsiang
chi*, where music and poetry—rather than action—are the chief
concern, Chin's many innovations may appear to some readers not
only uncalled for, but even preposterous. In most cases, he leaves
himself open to the accusation of imposing on the play things that
are alien to its intrinsic nature. Li Yü who, as we have seen above
in Chapter 1, praised profusely Chin's ability as a literary critic,
nevertheless pointed to this defective aspect in Chin's *Hsi-hsiang*
commentary: "In his commentary on *Hsi-hsiang*, Sheng-t'an can
be said to have scrutinized the most minute details, and exhausted
the most hidden significance: he has left no ideas in the play un-

explored. But in my opinion, his annotated *Hsi-hsiang* is fitting only for the perusal and amusement of literary men, but not for enactment by actors. The secret of literary writing Sheng-t'an has already acquired, but the secret of enacting he has yet to learn." [29] By "enactment" or "enacting," Li Yü is here referring to the technical aspects of singing and performing a play of this type.

Besides these meticulous, painstaking textual alterations, Chin also made two changes in the arrangement of the acts in the play. First, in the older edition, there are four Inductions (*hsieh-tzu*) [30] placed respectively before the first acts of Parts I, III, IV, and V. In Chin's edition, however, they are all incorporated into the acts immediately following. Second, Part II in the older edition has five acts.[31] In Chin's edition, on the other hand, it has only four acts, the first two acts being put together as one.

IV   *Appreciation of the Play as a Work of Art*

As in the case of the *Shui-hu chuan*, Chin lavished praise on the artistic achievement of the *Hsi-hsiang chi*. "*Hsi-hsiang chi* is no ordinary thing," he says in the first of his eighty-one notes on how to read the play. "It is [one of the most] marvelous (*miao*) [pieces of] writing between heaven and earth." [32] And as we have seen in Chin's discussion of the morality of the play in Section II above, it is on its literary qualities, not on its depiction of a secret love, that the merits of the play must be judged. For the sake of clarity and convenience, our discussion of this aspect of Chin's commentary can again be divided into sections.

A   *Superb Writing*

Two things about the writing in the play Chin praises constantly in his commentary. First, the author's ability to express or evoke a whole set of ideas or feelings in very few words, or in Chin's own picturesque way of speaking "one stroke of the brush serving the purpose of ten or a hundred strokes." [33] The two lines, "If you don't help me [secure a room],/I will blame you forever, Monk Fa Ts'ung!" is a good example. To illustrate this point more fully, however, let us cite two more examples.

In Part IV, Act I, Chang is waiting for the arrival of Ying-ying for their prearranged secret union, and he sings a series of lyrics expressing both his excitement and his anxiety. The first line in the first lyric runs thus: "I stand in expectation on these indifferent steps." [34] The expression "*chu li*" in the original, which is rendered "stand in expectation" here, also conveys the idea of a lapse of time. Chin commented on the line: "The lyrics coming after this all describe at length the fact of Ying-ying's not coming and Chang's waiting a long time. In this first line [of the first lyric], the author uses the expression *chu li*. This, then, indicates that Chang has already waited a long time, so that [the long waiting in] the following lyrics will appear even longer. . . . We can call this 'one group of words serving the purpose of two.' This is truly the secret of writing." [35] What Chin says here is that the author, instead of using a great many words to inform us that Chang has already stood on the steps for a long while, simply suggests it by the skillful use of the two words *chu li*, which reinforces at the same time Chang's long anxious wait described later.

In Part IV, Act III, after Chang Sheng has been ordered by Madame Ts'ui to travel to the capital to take the civil service examination, a farewell banquet is arranged in the Pavilion of Farewell. Chang Sheng has already gone ahead on a horse. Madame Ts'ui, Ying-ying, and Hung Niang now follow in a carriage. One of the lyrics sung by Ying-ying contains the following lines: "May his steed trot slowly,/And our carriage follow at a quicker pace." [36] Here the author has once again succeeded in revealing a complex psychological condition with just a few words. Chin was quick to seize the point. In a style that borders on tediousness, he tries to elucidate the richness of these two lines:

. . . These two sentences consisting of ten words are marvelous writing indeed. They depict vividly the complex state of mind which Ying-ying is in at this time, with all her childishness, naiveté, worry, and cleverness. For, since the interrogation of the day before, she has been separated from Chang Sheng for the entire night. Today she wants to take advantage of the farewell banquet to be with him again for a short while. But if Chang's horse goes quickly and her own carriage follows slowly, there will still be separation and they will not be able to be together for a longer time. Even if the horse goes slowly, and the carriage also follows slowly, or if the horse goes quickly and the carriage follows quickly, that still cannot be called being together. It is necessary for the horse to go slowly, and the carriage to follow quickly. If the carriage follows quickly while the horse goes slowly, then the cariage will be at the right of the horse, and the horse at the left of the carriage. Thus Chang will be on the left and Ying-ying on the right, riding together side by side. . . .[37]

    The second thing Chin praises is the author's skill in indirect exposition. This technique Chin himself characterizes as "Painting the clouds to bring into relief the moon" (*hung yun t'o yueh*), a technical term in Chinese painting, whose significance Chin explains thus: "One wants to paint the moon, but cannot paint it directly, he therefore paints the clouds [around it]. Although he paints in the clouds, his mind is not on the clouds. The reason why his mind is not on the clouds is that it is on the moon." [38] This is a favorite artistic device in China, one that is clearly inspired by the teachings of Taoism and Buddhism. According to both ideologies, the highest form of truth is not something that can be described or talked about directly; it can only be hinted at or suggested indirectly.
    Chin was apparently very fond of this literary technique. Five of the eighty-one notes he provided on how to read the play deal specifically with it.[39] The main argument in these notes can be summarized as follows: although it is essential for a writer to have a theme or point of emphasis in his writing, it need not be, and indeed is better not, stated or pointed out explicitly. A first-rate writer, such as the author of the *Hsi-hsiang chi*, is the one who will try to explore his theme from various perspectives and use all the rhetorical devices at his command. He will, in other words, circle around his main point in all possible ways, and never quite approach it directly, leaving that as a task for the reader. Good writing is "clearly like a circus lion rolling a ball. The main thing is just the ball. The lion is nevertheless made to exhibit all of its tricks. In a moment, all the people in the tent begin to watch the lion until their eyes become dazzled. The lion, however, is not concerned. While the eyes of the people are concentrating on it, its own eyes are concentrating on the ball. This is because the one who rolls the ball is the lion, and the reason why it rolls in this way and in that way is in truth all because of the ball." [40] Chin concludes, "The *Tso-chuan* and *Shih-chi* employ this method exclusively; so does the *Hsi-hsiang chi*." [41]
    Chin thought so highly of this technique that he himself used it extensively in his commentary. In his Introductory Remarks to

Part IV, Act II, for example, in order to express the joy he felt in
reading the act, he begins by recalling the "Thirty-three Delights
in Life" he and a friend had counted together while staying at an
inn.[42] This, in a way, accounts for his sometimes seemingly clumsy,
roundabout way of presenting his points in the commentary. As
we will see presently, Chin's concept of this technique also constitutes the basis of his taking Ying-ying to be the central figure in
the play, and of his arguing for the play to end properly after Part
IV.

B *Ying-ying Is the Central Figure*

In a Yüan dynasty play such as the *Hsi-hsiang chi*, singing roles
are usually restricted to the leading characters only, and the degree of importance of any leading character can be judged by the
number of arias he is required to sing. Seen in such a light, the
leading characters in the *Hsi-hsiang chi* are Ying-ying, Chang
Sheng, and Hung Niang. Of the three, Ying-ying is the least important, having to sing fewer arias than the other two.[43] Chin
agrees that Ying-ying, Chang Sheng, and Hung Niang are the
leading characters, for he writes: "*Hsi-hsiang chi* writes only
about three persons. One is Shuang-wen (*i.e.* Ying-ying), one is
Chang Sheng, and one is Hung Niang. The rest . . . are merely
tools incidentally employed when the other three are being portrayed." [44] But Chin has a different idea with regard to the relative
importance of the three. To him, Ying-ying is unquestionably the
central figure in the entire play. "If we consider the matter more
carefully," he says, "*Hsi-hsiang chi* was written solely for the purpose of describing one person. This one person is none other than
Shuang-wen herself. . . ." [45] And he illustrates Ying-ying's relationship with the other two by two elaborate and rather amusing
similes:

To draw a comparison from writing, Ying-ying is the theme, Chang
Sheng the text, and Hung Niang the introduction, the continuation, the
shift of point of view, and the summing up of the essay. Because of the
many uses of an introduction, a continuation, a shift in point of view,
and a summing up, the theme will appear from the text and the text
will be merged into the theme. . . .[46]

To draw a comparison from the act of preparing medicine, Chang
Sheng is the sickness, Ying-ying, the herb, and Hung Niang, the

decocting of the herb. Because of frequent decocting, the herb will come to the help of the sickness and the sickness will approach the herb. . . .[47]

Chin recognizes the importance of Chang Sheng and Hung Niang, but for him Ying-ying is still the main "theme," the healing "medicine," in short, the protagonist.

If Ying-ying is the central figure in the play, then why did the author not give her more arias to sing? Chin did not raise the question in exactly this way. Instead, he asked: Why does the play not begin with Ying-ying singing, but instead with Chang Sheng? (In fact, Ying-ying not only does not sing in the first act, but even throughout the entire first part.) His own answer is that the author here is using the technique of "Painting the clouds to bring into relief the moon":

> The creation of Hsi-hsiang is solely for the sake of Shuang-wen. However, Shuang-wen is a national beauty, and a national beauty cannot be painted and refined simply by buying lots of cosmetics. Moreover, Shuang-wen is a heavenly creature, and a heavenly creature cannot be touched up or modeled by a petty artisan of this lowly earth. The author wants to portray Shuang-wen, but cannot do it; so he puts her aside, and first writes about Chang Sheng. This is the secret recipe of the painter's so-called "Painting the clouds to bring into relief the moon."[48]

We do not have to agree with Chin's answer to the question. Indeed, we do not even have to agree with his taking Ying-ying to be the central figure in the play. But the very fact that Chin could raise an artistic question and then attempt to answer it at all, and that he did maintain a critical position on the relative importance of the characters in the play does reveal his acumen as a critic in this initial stage of drama and fiction criticism in China.

Chin not only considered Ying-ying the protagonist in the play, but also showed great admiration for her as a person. To him, she represented the ideal of a perfect young lady, not only beautiful but also well-bred and well-educated. She was, as we have seen above, "a national beauty," "a heavenly creature." She "was truly a well-behaved young lady from the family of a Chief Minister."[49] In order to preserve such an image of Ying-ying throughout the play, Chin again resorted to his old trick of tampering with the text. Any word, line, or even passage in the play, that seemed in contradiction with this image, was either ingeniously altered or simply struck out.[50] As we will see in Section D below, one of Chin's main objections to Part V is that it depicts Ying-ying in too vulgar a light. For the moment, let us cite two examples as illustration.

In the very first act of Part I, when Ying-ying and Hung Niang chance to run into the stranger Chang Sheng in the monastery, they turn back, leaving Chang in a state of confusion and bewilderment. In the older edition, when the three meet each other, it is Hung Niang who proposes to go back home.

Hung Niang says:
    Young Mistress, there is someone over there, let's
        go back home.
    (Ying-ying turns, casts a glance at Chang, and exits.)[51]

There is strong indication in the action of Ying-ying that she is rather attracted by the handsome young scholar. To Chin, however, this would seem to be an improper thing for a well-behaved young lady to do. He therefore changed the lines as follows:

Ying-ying says:
    Hung Niang, I am going back to see Mother.[52]

Not only does Ying-ying become the one who takes the initiative by proposing to go back, but the stage direction stating that she looks back at Chang is eliminated. As though not yet quite satisfied with the change, Chin added by way of commentary: "I don't know whether Ying-ying has seen Chang Sheng on this day or not. . . . Some stupid editors insist that Ying-ying at this moment has already tried to incite Chang Sheng with her eyes and heart, and other ugly gestures! How could they be capable of appreciating what magnificent writing the *Hsi-hsiang chi* really is!"[53]

Similarly in Part I, Act IV, during a religious service in memory of Ying-ying's father, the script in the older edition runs as follows:

The Monk says:
    The wind has blown out the candles.

Chang says:
    Let me light them up, and burn the incense.
Ying-ying speaks to Hung Niang:
    That young scholar has been busy the whole night.
She sings:
    Outside he appears romantic, young and in his
        prime,
    Inside he is intelligent, matchless in his
        study and talent.
    Twining this way and that, he makes a hundred vain gestures,
    Pacing to and fro, he shows off his smartness before
        others.
Hung Niang says:
    I think that young scholar . . .
. . . .
Chang says:
    How the young lady looks at my humble self! [54]

All of this is expurgated from Chin's edition, for the obvious reason that it appears to him inappropriate that a dignified, well-
educated young lady should appear so flirtatious during a solemn
religious ceremony, even though Ying-ying has by now already
declared her feelings to Chang Sheng.

As a result of these revisions and excisions, the somewhat
simple, straightforward, warmhearted Ying-ying in the older edition becomes in Chin's edition a more delicate, refined, and so-
phisticated creature who, instead of falling in love with a stranger
at the very first encounter (as the older edition seems to suggest),
allows her love for Chang to proceed impalpably from a state of
seeming casualness in the beginning to great intensity in the end.[55]
In short, Chin's Ying-ying becomes more typically a traditional
Chinese lady from a good family.

C The Structure of the Play and Related Questions

While the novel *Shui-hu chuan* is episodic in structure, the play
Hsi-hsiang chi shows a remarkable degree of unity and tightness
in its overall organization as a work of art. Chin was aware of this
fact. In his Introductory Remarks to Part III, Act IV, he gives a
full description of the play's structure. Since it is impossible to
summarize his statement in a few words, I shall translate the main
part of it here:[56]

. . . As for the sixteen acts[57] in the *Hsi-hsiang chi,* I can truly say that in them there is [a thing called] "budding forth" (*sheng*) and there is [a thing called] "sweeping away" (*sao*). "Budding forth" is like the budding forth of leaves and flowers, and "sweeping away" is like the sweeping away of the leaves and flowers. . . . But what is meant by "budding forth" and "sweeping away" in the *Hsi-hsiang chi?* The first act, "Beauty's Enchantment," can be called the "budding forth" and the last act,[58] "A Feast with Tears," can be called the "sweeping away." For before "Beauty's Enchantment," there is no *Hsi-hsiang chi* . . . it is simply a great void. After "A Feast with Tears," there is also no *Hsi-hsiang chi* . . . it is again a great void. This is the greatest organizing principle of the *Hsi-hsiang chi.* In between these two acts, there are "this one arrives" (*tz'u lai*) and "that one arrives" (*pi lai*). What is meant by "this one arrives"? In the act, "The Renting of the Quarters in the Monastery" (Part I, Act II) Chang Sheng appears. This is called "this one arrives." What is meant by "that one arrives"? In the act, "A Poem and Its Response" (Part I, Act III) Ying-ying appears. This is called "that one arrives." . . . If Chang Sheng did not rent a room in the monastery, it would be a case of his not appearing. If Chang Sheng did not appear there would be no "budding forth" of the story. Granted that Chang Sheng had rented the room, but if Ying-ying did not respond to Chang's poem, this would be a case of her not appearing. If Ying-ying did not appear, there would still be no "budding forth" of the story. Now, since Chang Sheng appears on account of Ying-ying's beauty, and Ying-ying appears on account of Chang Sheng's talent . . . in between the two there has already developed a thin thread secretly binding them together and a gentle spirit causing them to communicate with each other. Without realizing it, they are already caught helplessly by the force of love. Then there are the "three stages of development" (*san-chien*, lit. "the three graduals"). What is meant by "three stages of development"? "The Interruption of the Religious Service" (Part I, Act IV) is the first stage. "The Alarm at the Monastery" (Part II, Act I) is the second stage. The present scene (*i.e.* Part III, Act IV), "Further Expectations," is the third stage. In the first stage, Ying-ying sees Chang Sheng for the first time. In the second stage, Ying-ying begins to be concerned with Chang Sheng. In the third stage, Ying-ying begins to allow Chang Sheng to consider her as a lover . . . Then there are the "two tentatives" (*erh-chin*, lit. "approaches") and "three withdrawals" (*san-tsung*). What are the "tentatives"? "The Invitation to the Feast" (Part II, Act II) is the first tentative. "First Expectations" (Part III, Act I) is the second tentative. The idea of "tentative" is that one is almost about to get something. The idea that one is almost about to get something is that in the end he does not get it. One does not

get it in the end, and yet it is written as though he is almost about
to get it—this is the method of producing suspense and variety in composition. As for the "three withdrawals," "The Breach of Promise"
(Part II, Act III) is one, "Repudiation of the Billet-doux" (Part III,
Act III) is another, and "Hung Niang in the Dock" (Part IV, Act II)
is the third. If there is something tentative, there is bound to be withdrawal. In order to keep two people far apart, they are brought close
together. In order to bring two people close together, they are kept far
apart. The idea of withdrawal is that one is almost about to lose something. The idea that one is almost about to lose something is that in
the end he does not lose it. One does not lose it in the end, and yet it
is written as though he is almost about to lose it—this is the method
of producing suspense and variety in composition. . . . Then there are
two "cannot-but-be-so's" (*pu te pu jan*). What are the two "cannot-but-
be-so's"? "Love and the Lute" (Part II, Act IV) cannot but be so, and
"The Fuss about the Billet-doux" (Part III, Act II) cannot but be so.
In "Love and the Lute" it is Hung Niang who cannot but be so. In
"The Fuss about the Billet-doux" it is Ying-ying who cannot but be so.
If it were not so in "Love and the Lute," then Hung Niang would not
be Hung Niang. If Hung Niang were not Hung Niang, then Ying-ying
would not be Ying-ying. Why is this so? Because Ying-ying could then
be blamed for acting like a common weaving girl sighing by the door,
so that her mother would find out the secret. If it were not so in "The
Fuss about the Billet-doux," then Ying-ying would not be Ying-ying.
If Ying-ying were not Ying-ying, then Chang Sheng would not be
Chang Sheng. Why is this so? Because Chang Sheng could then be
blamed for acting like someone of humble origin who upon returning
home would immediately embrace his lover without suspecting that
lustful fellows would take great delight in such a thing.[59] Then there
is an act of "solid writing," where the numberless words of the book,
turning this way and that with all their ramifications, all converge . . .
as in the next act, "The Fulfilment of the Billet-doux." Then there is
also an act of "empty writing," where the numberless words of the
book, turning this way and that with all their ramifications, all become
completely useless here . . . as in the last act, "A Surprising Dream."
All of these then are what is meant by the writing of the *Hsi-hsiang
chi*—sixteen acts in all. But I can truly say that to call it (*i.e.* the writing) sixteen acts is possible, to call it one act is also possible; to say
that hundreds of thousands of words all congregate here is possible,
to say that it (again referring to the writing of *Hsi-hsiang*) is devoid
of any trace of ink is also possible.

This is a very important piece of criticism. It states in a nutshell
Chin's whole critique of the play as a work of art. His great admi-

ration for the literary style of the play is reiterated. To him, the writing cannot be characterized in any ordinary way, it is in truth indefinable. In its supreme literary quality, it has, like the highest form of truth, achieved something of a transcendent entity which refuses any finite categorization. It is everything ("hundreds of thousands of words all congregate here"), it is nothing ("it is devoid of any trace of ink"). But what is even of more interest, the above passage clearly shows that in his critical analysis of the play Chin is not just concerned with individual words or lyrical effects, though they form a large portion of his commentary. In his attention to minute details, he never loses sight of the overall pattern. He is fully aware of the suspense and tension in the action, which form the basis of the structure of the play as a whole.

Related to his structural analysis of the play are two highly significant artistic questions Chin raises and then answers in his commentary. Here again we, as modern readers, may not want wholly to accept his answers. But when viewed in proper historical perspective, Chin must be given credit for having even asked such questions. In fact, one wishes he had asked more. The first such question occurs in the Introductory Remarks to Part II, Act III. To paraphrase Chin: Why—since this is the scene in which Madame Ts'ui is to repudiate her promise that Ying-ying and Chang Sheng can marry—are the lyrics in the act not sung by her or by someone else, but instead by Ying-ying? If we, as modern readers, were to tackle such a question, we would naturally go to the structure of the entire play for a possible answer. We would find that the assignment of the singing part to Ying-ying in this scene is highly appropriate. The author wanted to show the kind of psychological reaction Ying-ying would undoubtedly go through upon hearing her mother's verdict on her future. She is deeply upset when she hears her mother bid her and Chang Sheng to address each other as brother and sister, but not as husband and wife. A sense of rebellion, though perhaps unconscious at the moment, begins to be engendered in her heart. This is a very important fact in that it prepares Ying-ying psychologically to act as she does a few scenes later, taking the initiative in going to meet Chang Sheng in his room. Until now, Chang Sheng has been the one to take the initiative in gaining the attention of Ying-ying. After this scene, however, he is completely at the end of his wits. He has done his very best, and the final step in their relationship

will have to be taken by Ying-ying herself. Without this scene, in
which we see how Ying-ying is mortified by her mother, how
deeply she loves Chang Sheng and how she is genuinely moved
by Chang Sheng's plight, the step she takes a few scenes later
would appear quite incomprehensible.

Chin's own answer seems to have to do with the matter of literary decorum. Madame Ts'ui, Chin maintains, should not sing because, under the circumstances, her words would sound "antago-
nistic" (*fan*). Nor should Chang Sheng sing because, in his state
of great agitation, his words would sound "violent" (*chi*). Hung
Niang should not sing either because her words would be "incomplete" (*pan*) (*i.e.* being a mere maid she could not very well express everything she wanted to say). What is left, then, is for Ying-
ying to sing, as she should because (being an obedient daughter
and a devoted lover) she can express herself completely (*chin*)
and yet in an agreeable manner (*wan*).[60]

Chin's second question is posed in his Introductory Remarks to
Part III, Act III. Chang Sheng has just sent a love letter to Ying-
ying through Hung Niang. Although Ying-ying pretends to be en-
raged when she sees it, she nevertheless responds with a verse sug-
gesting a rendezvous at night (Part III, Act II). Elated by such a
happy turn of events, Chang sets out for the appointment only to
meet a stern rebuff from Ying-ying (Part III, Act III). Chin's
question then is, to paraphrase him again: Why should Ying-ying
get angry after seeing Chang's letter, and above all turn him back
mercilessly after having enticed him to come secretly by sending
him a highly suggestive verse? To answer this question, Chin
makes a perceptive and illuminating probe into Ying-ying's character. "Shuang-wen (Ying-ying)," says Chin, "is the most dignified . . . the most affectionate . . . the most clever . . . and
the proudest girl in the world." [61] Her deep love for Chang Sheng,
Chin suggests, naturally makes her happy to see Chang's open
expression of love in the form of a letter, and she even responds to
it by inviting him over for a secret union. Yet, being a highly
clever and sensitive girl, she cannot but suspect that Chang
Sheng, in his desperate effort to seek Hung Niang's help, has
probably already confided everything to the latter. Her suspicion
is made all the stronger when she notices the casualness and mischievousness with which Hung Niang has begun to treat her
lately. She resents all this, because she believes the love between

herself and Chang should be treated with utter privacy and re-spect, and should not be revealed in all its details to a third party. Her dignity, and above all her pride, Chin continues, are wounded; hence, her seemingly contradictory action.[62]

D   *The Problem of Part V*

Chin's view on the last part of the play is also related to his concept of the structure of the play. But since to expound his view fully would involve a discussion of the authorship of the play, we shall deal with it in this section.

Various views have been advanced with regard to the author-ship of the play. In his article "*Hsi-hsiang chi* hsü-shuo" (Notes on the *Hsi-hsiang chi*),[63] Wang Chi-szu, an authority on the play, groups these views into four categories: (1) Kuan Han-ch'ing (*fl.* 1246) wrote the entire play; (2) Wang Shih-fu (*fl.* 1300) wrote the entire play; (3) Wang Shih-fu wrote the first four parts, the fifth one being a continuation by Kuan; (4) Vice versa.[64] Wang then proceeds to show convincingly why he does not believe the last part (Part V) to be a continuation, and why he thinks the whole play is in fact the work of Wang Shih-fu alone. Among the bits of evidence and reasons enumerated by Wang to support his argument, we need only point out the three most important. First, historically the *Hsi-hsiang chi* is closely modeled upon Tung Chieh-yuan's medley *Hsi-hsiang ch'ou-t'an-tz'u*. In Tung's work, the story ends with a happy marriage between Chang Sheng and Ying-ying, the description of which forms the main part of Part V in *Hsi-hsiang chi*.[65] Second, both the *Lu kuei pu* and the *T'ai-ho cheng-yin p'u*, the two earliest bibliographies of Yuan dynasty plays, attribute the *Hsi-hsiang chi* to Wang Shih-fu.[66] Third, stylis-tically the *Hsi-hsiang chi* is more typical of Wang Shih-fu's writ-ing than of Kuan Han-ch'ing's.[67] Wang Chi-szu's view on the authorship of the *Hsi-hsiang chi* is generally shared by modern scholars.[68]

As we have already seen above in the long translated passage on the structure of the *Hsi-hsiang chi* (IV C), Chin took the play to be in four parts with a total of sixteen acts. In his Introductory Remarks to Part V, Act I, he further makes it clear that he consid-ered this last part a continuation. "These four supplementary acts of the *Hsi-hsiang chi*," says he, "came I don't know from whose hand." [69] Although he does not specify Kuan Han-ch'ing's name here, it is clear that his position in the controversy over the authorship of the play belongs essentially to the third category listed above. Chin of course did not start the "continuation" rumor. According to Wang Chi-szu, the first man to start such a rumor was Hsü Shih-fan, who flourished around 1580, about half a century earlier than Chin's time. But because of the unsurpassed popularity of Chin's edition of the *Hsi-hsiang chi*, his became more or less the orthodox view among later scholars.[70]

Now, it would be an easy matter to discredit Chin's effort to put aside the last part of the play as something unauthentic by simply citing all the evidence already marshaled by Wang Chi-szu. To do so, however, would be unfair to Chin. Unlike the *Shui-hu chuan*, where he simply cut short the story without further ado, here he still kept the last part in its entirety, and even continued to provide elaborate, albeit mostly abusive, comments for it. Moreover, whereas his drastic truncation of the novel was apparently politically motivated, his present stand was largely based on esthetic considerations. First he explained why he thought the play should end after Part IV, Act IV. Actually he even felt that the play could have ended one act earlier, *i.e.* after Part IV, Act III, as we have seen above in (IV C): ". . . before 'Beauty's Enchantment' (Part I, Act I), there is no *Hsi-hsiang chi*; it is simply a great void. After 'A Feast with Tears' (Part IV, Act III), there is also no *Hsi-hsiang chi*; it is again a great void. This is the greatest organizing principle of the *Hsi-hsiang chi*." But Wang Shih-fu wrote one more act ("A Surprising Dream") after this. Why? Chin's answer to this question again betrays his deep immersion in Buddhist teachings. To him, as to any philosopher-Buddhist, life is but a big dream, a complete illusion. "Now," he said, "heaven and earth constitute the country of Dream, and the mass of people the souls of dreams." [71] By ending the play with a dream in which Chang Sheng dreams about Ying-ying in a lonely inn on his way to the capital to take the examination, so Chin implies, Wang Shih-fu wants to drive home this important message to the reader. According to Chin, then, this is the *raison d'être* of Act IV of Part IV.[72]

Then he offered two cogent arguments as to why he deemed Part V of the play artistically superfluous: First, the last part, compared to the preceding ones, is much inferior in quality. The description of Ying-ying in the first act of this part, for instance, fails to accord with the fact that she is the daughter of a Chief Minister. Having been separated from Chang Sheng for only half a year, she loses all the poise and self-restraint of a dignified young lady. She forgets the importance of the nature of Chang's journey to the capital, while being seemingly unmoved by the very good tidings of his success in the highest literary examination. "All she knows is that it is hard to stay alone in an empty bed. She whines and howls to no end. Thus [our image of] a gifted beauty and a talented scholar at this point is completely swept away." [73] Secondly, the best kind of writing is that which turns this way and that way until it has come to the most vital part (Chang Sheng's marriage with Ying-ying in this case). But once the vital part is reached, it must stop without any further ado. To try to describe the vital part would be like painting the lower half of the picture of a beautiful woman whose upper half has already been skillfully done. It is not only unnecessary but truly to be despised. Part V of the *Hsi-hsiang chi* is thus the lower half of the picture of a beautiful woman.[74]

It should be noted that by thus ending the play after Part IV, Chin does not necessarily have in mind a tragic ending for the play, as some scholars would like to believe.[75] The idea of life as a dream is in itself a philosophical attitude, not necessarily one carrying any tragic overtones. From his other arguments, Chin's position is rather: since everything in the play thus far already points to a final union between Ying-ying and Chang Sheng, why waste more effort to depict in detail such a union? Chin makes himself even clearer in his comments on the last act of Part V. Toward the very end of Part V, Chang Sheng, after formally marrying Ying-ying, sings a lyric to express his happiness. Chin's comment reads: "The four supplementary acts specially designed above are all, I suppose, for the sake of these few lines. [The author of the supplement] has wasted a great deal of energy, and yet these few lines are carelessly done. I really don't see why he wanted to do so." [76] What is important here is that Chin does not say whether the supplement has spoiled the tragic atmosphere in the main part of the play or not, but simply that it is *unnecessary*.

V *The Same Highly Individual Style*

In Section V of Chapter 3 above, we dwelt at some length on the highly individual style of Chin's *Shui-hu* commentary. What has been said there can apply equally to his *Hsi-hsiang* commentary. True, his old ebullience seems toned down somewhat, and he becomes on the whole more relaxed and philosophical.[77] But the basically witty, loquacious, and fun-loving Chin is still unmistakably there. Even in his brief remarks on how best to appreciate the play, we see his wit, his darting imagination, and his humor—that is his peculiar style and genius:

Reading the *Hsi-hsiang chi*, one must sweep the floor [first]. The reason for sweeping the floor is that one must not cherish even one bit of dirt in one's mind.

Reading the *Hsi-hsiang chi*, one must burn incense. The reason for burning incense is to show respect so that one can be in communion with ghosts and spirits.

Reading the *Hsi-hsiang chi*, one must sit in front of snow. The reason for doing this is that snow will enhance the book's purity and cleanness.

Reading the *Hsi-hsiang chi*, one must sit in front of a flower. The reason for doing this is that the flower will increase the book's gracefulness and beauty.

Reading the *Hsi-hsiang chi*, one must sit side by side with a beautiful lady. The reason for doing this is to experience the book's moving sentiments.

Reading the *Hsi-hsiang chi*, one must sit in front of a Taoist priest. The reason for doing this is to sigh over the fact that there is no way of escape [from the toils of love].[78]

Certainly half of the fun of reading the *Hsi-hsiang* commentary would be gone if we did not frequently come into close contact with such an original, if somewhat unrestrained, mind.

CHAPTER 6

Commentary on Tu Fu

T U FU (712–770) is generally considered to be China's greatest poet. In selecting him as a man of genius, Chin was for once being conventional in his judgment. Ironically, however, his critical analysis of one hundred and eighty-odd poems of the poet is less well known than his commentaries on the *Shui-hu chuan* and *Hsi-hsiang chi*.[1] In Ch'iu Chao-ao's authoritative 1713 edition of Tu-Fu's poems, for example, which is said to contain "the most minute explanations of Tu Fu's allusions and the fullest discussions of his poetics, both of which Ch'ou selected from previous masters accessible to him," [2] Chin's name, as far as I can tell, is not mentioned even once. This is perhaps understandable, because, while in his commentaries on the *Shui-hu chuan* and *Hsi-hsiang chi* he was doing what few others had done before him, in his analysis of Tu Fu's poetry he was working in a well-established tradition in which originality cannot easily be seen; secondly, and perhaps more importantly, his name had become so inseparable from the *Shui-hu chuan* and *Hsi-hsiang chi* that he was invariably the "heretic" in the eyes of many "orthodox" scholars, and therefore his comments on poetry, though full of insight and quite unique, were passed over in silence.

I *Critical Procedure*

Chin's procedure in analyzing the poems is similar to that in his two previous works. Before each poem there is usually a brief introduction which contains critical remarks on the poem as a whole. With the exception of poems of the *chüeh-chü* (quatrain) type, which are too short (just four lines) to be broken up, each poem is further divided into some self-contained sections, with comments following each section. Poems of the Regulated Verse type are invariably divided into two sections, with each section comprising four lines. In the case of longer poems, the number of sections is not fixed. The famous long narrative poem "The Trip North" (Pei cheng), for example, is divided into thirty-five small sections.

Few people would quarrel with Chin over the feasibility of cutting a longer poem into several sections—if only because this does facilitate discussion. But his regular practice of dividing a Regulated Verse poem into two equal parts is a different matter altogether. Because of its brevity (eight lines in all), a Regulated Verse poem usually forms a tight unit which cannot always be cut into two separate parts. Even when it can, the dividing line does not always fall in the middle of the poem. Such a practice must have aroused unfavorable criticism from his contemporaries, since he complained to a friend, "This matter [of cutting a Regulated Verse poem into two equal parts] should be easy to see, and yet it has met with approval from no one." [3] To defend himself, all kinds of arguments were put forward.[4] Perhaps the most cogent argument is that this was intended as a countermeasure against widespread malpractices in contemporary verse.

The Regulated Verse became an established form with the beginning of the T'ang Dynasty (618–907). The metrical rules governing its composition required that the four middle lines form two antithetical couplets, contrasting with each other in sense as well as in sound. Since to achieve the required effect called for greater effort and ingenuity than the composition of an ordinary line, as time went on, practitioners of this type of poetry began to pay attention to the four middle lines only. Once the two couplets were composed, the poem was considered finished, with the addition of the remaining lines merely a perfunctory requirement.[5] Being a critic who emphasized the importance of every part of the whole, Chin was naturally appalled by this kind of slipshod writing. By dividing the poem into two equal parts and paying equal attention to both, he hoped to exert a corrective influence on contemporary poetic practice. Thus, he said:

Since a [Regulated Verse] poem originally took eight lines as its rule, how can I analyze it by forcibly dividing it into two parts? It should be known that I am not trying to grow an ulcer on a piece of wholesome meat: I am simply suiting the remedy to the disease. When the T'ang poets prescribed eight lines [for the Regulated Verse], it originally meant to take two lines as "beginning" (ch'i), two lines as "continuation" (*ch'eng*), two lines as "shift in meaning" (*chuan*), and two lines as "summation" (*ho*).[6] This is a fixed rule. Then [some T'ang poets] simply made the first and last couplets metrically more flexible, while regarding it a merit to have two fine antithetical couplets in the middle. Consequently, later poets began to follow the set pattern and vainly to compete for what is fine and delicate, while ignoring the main meaning [of the poem]. When people write poetry of late, they go so far as to take the middle four lines to be the main body of the poem, and then insert two lines at the front as the beginning and add two lines to the end as the conclusion. . . . How would they know that lines three and four solely continue lines one and two, and that the meaning of the latter is high and lofty and [their organization] stricter than the former; and that lines five and six yield lines seven and eight, and that the latter are subtle and deep and yet more moving than the former? How can they use the two words "beginning" and "conclusion" to obliterate the countless efforts of the ancients? For this reason, I do not mind being quarrelsome, or to analyze a poem by dividing it [into two parts]. Those who blame me say that a poem is originally a single entity, so how can it be split into two sections? But those who know me say that in my analysis of a poem, when divided into sections, the poem actually becomes one; and that in the murky analysis of others, when the sections are put together, the poem actually splits apart. . . . This is why I cannot but argue earnestly even at the risk of being ridiculed. A thousand years later my effort may be appreciated.[7]

This is well said (even though somewhat forcedly). Still we may question whether in his effort to combat one extreme he has not gone to another.

II   *Tu Fu as a Poet*

In examining Chin's commentary on Tu Fu's poetry, we are handicapped by the fact that it is unfinished, and that there are no prefaces or explanatory notes (as is the case with the *Shui-hu* and *Hsi-hsiang* commentaries) in which he offers his assessment of Tu Fu's achievement as a whole. His comments on individual poems, then, will be our sole guide in this part of our discussion.

In his commentary, Chin seems particularly to admire three things about Tu Fu as a poet. First, Tu Fu's ability to describe a thing, an event, or an action vividly. Chin's formulaic expressions in this regard are "like a picture" (*ju-hua*), "to paint a vivid picture of it" (*huo hua-ch'u-lai*), etc. In his commentary on the *Shui-*

hu chuan, it will be recalled, Chin praised Shih Nai-an in precisely
the same way. However, there seems to be one important difference in this case: whereas in the novel vividness is achieved
through minute, detailed, and realistic descriptions, in Tu Fu's
poetry it is the result of the selection of a few carefully chosen but
representative details. Thus, in praise of Tu Fu's vivid style, Chin
is more likely to say, "A vivid picture is painted with just so many
words," or something to this effect.

In his discussion of this aspect of Tu Fu's style, Chin makes an
interesting distinction between the word *"chìng"* (a scene) and
the word *"chǐng"* (scenery). While "scenery" describes merely
the external appearance of a thing, a "scene" conveys the mood or
inner spirit of a thing. "A scene is different from a piece of scenery," he states. "The latter is noisy (*nao*) while the former is quiet
(*ching*); scenery is near (*chin*), but a scene is far (*yuan*); the
former lies in front of shallow people and the latter resides in the
inner vision of profound individuals." [8] To Chin, Tu Fu is a
superb poet not only because he could paint vivid sceneries, but
far more importantly, because he could create memorable scenes,
as Chin's comments on the poem "Visiting the Feng-hsien Monastery at Lung-men" (Yu Lung-men Feng-hsien Szu) clearly indicate:

> Earlier I visited the grounds with the monks,
> Now I have spent the night in the monastery.
> The music of stillness rises in the dark ravine,
> The radiance of moonlight is filtered through the forest.
> The Heaven's Gap seems to press upon the constellations.
> Sleep among the clouds has chilled my clothes.
> The early prayer bell struck as I was about to wake,
> Am I awake with my soul as well as my senses? [9]

Although the word "visiting" does appear in the title of the poem,
the poem itself depicts not what the poet saw during a daylight
tour, but rather a night scene after the tour. Why is this so?

Could it be that this poem is meant as a supplement to describe
things after the visit? If so, could it be that originally the poet had
thought of two poems under the same title, but the first poem was
forgotten. I thought about this problem over and over again, but to
no avail. One day while I was sitting idly with nothing to do, I sud-

denly hit upon the answer: Truly Mr. Tu Fu is here teaching us the lesson that in composing a poem we must not write carelessly. For example, if he had started to write at random while in the middle of the tour, of course he could have produced a poem. But the [memorable] scenes of a dark ravine and a moonlit forest would never have been touched upon. If no such [memorable] scenes are touched upon in a poem, it will not affect the reader, and if the poem one writes does not affect the reader, it is as good as not having been written at all. For this reason Mr. Tu Fu . . . used the word "visiting" in the title of the poem, but the poem itself was not written until after he had stayed overnight in the monastery. This way he was able to get rid of all the superficial expressions, clichés, and vulgar words likely to be used by ordinary visitors to the monastery, and, employing a different device, to write a refreshingly new piece. That Tu Fu's poetry has been considered the best in a thousand years is truly no vain praise! [10]

Conciseness is another thing about Tu Fu's poetry which greatly appeals to Chin. "With only ten words (*i.e.* in the original) the poet has described completely the affairs of that time," is his comment on a couplet from one of two poems called "The Past" (Su hsi) about the infatuation of the Emperor Ming-huang (reigned 713–756) with Lady Yang: "A haughty flower facing a motley bunch of trees,/A delighted dragon coming out of a smooth pool." [11] The "haughty flower" represents Lady Yang lording it over the other ladies of the court, who are described as "a motley bunch of trees," while the "dragon" of course refers to the Emperor himself. In much the same way Chin praises the following couplet from a poem in which the poet expresses his great joy in anticipation of the imminent arrival of his younger brother: "In times of chaos life is full of separations;/My illness should be cured when we meet again." "In times of chaos," Chin comments, "there is separation even while alive; so it is only understandable that death may occur after separation. Now all of a sudden two brothers are going to meet together. What a boundless joy this is! Can there still be an incurable illness? Within the scope of just ten words countless turns and twists of meaning can be detected. You will see the point if you turn the couplet over carefully in your mind." [12] Of course, conciseness is something to be found in all good poetry. But there is no question in Chin's mind that this is an especially noteworthy feature of Tu Fu's poetry, as can be seen in the comments on the first two lines of a poem entitled "Shown to Tsung-wen and Tsung-wu on the Cooked Food Festival" (Shu-shih jih shih Tsung-wen Tsung-wu): "Roaming along the Yangtze and the Han River afflicted with diabetes,/I am detained in my lodging as war rages all about." And Chin's comments read: "Our poet was ill during his travels, and could not return home for years. Wasn't this on account of war? These initial ten words (*i.e.* in the original) are matched together in an extremely complex way. Countless ink would have been wasted had they come from other people's hands." [13]

Finally, what Chin admires about Tu Fu is his highly subtle and suggestive style. In his comments on a poem called "A Night Abroad" (K'e yeh), after praising Tu Fu's skill in portraying the sleepless night of a troubled traveler in the first four lines of the poem:

> Sleeping abroad, how can I close my eyes?
> The autumn sky begrudges turning light.
> As the remnants of the setting moon penetrate through the door screen,
> High on my pillow I hear the river in the distance.

he concludes admiringly, "Not once is the word 'miserable' used in these four lines, and yet the feeling of misery they convey is boundless." [14] Similarly, in his comments on the fifth of a series of nine quatrains known as "Miscellaneous Feelings" (Man-hsing):

> It is heartbreaking to realize the spring is about to end on the riverside!
> I halt my stroll to lean on my staff and view the exuberant beach:
> Mad catkins of willow dancing with the breeze;
> Fickle blossoms of the peach drifting with the stream.

Chin remarks, "This poem says that spring is about to disappear after all. Time truly flows away very fast. What is so marvelous about the whole poem, however, is that it does not state [directly] that spring is about to go away, but instead says the river is about to end (a more literal rendering of the first line would be "I am heart-broken to see the spring river about to come to an end"). . . . There hasn't been much such marvelous writing." [15]

What Chin is saying here is actually a restatement of his favorite esthetic principle already discussed above in the chapter on the *Hsi-hsiang chi,* namely, "Painting the clouds to bring into relief the moon." Chin attached so much value to this principle, which can also be called the principle of indirection, that he declared rather emphatically in comments on another poem by Tu Fu, "Direct writing is never as good as indirect writing."[16] To Chin, therefore, Tu Fu is another of those great literary masters who excel in their ability to depict things subtly and indirectly.

The qualities Chin admired in Tu Fu as we have seen so far all have to do with style and writing technique. While admiring Tu Fu as a superb craftsman, however, Chin showed equal respect for him as a person. Throughout the commentary Chin constantly calls attention to Tu Fu as a good friend, a devoted son, an affectionate father and husband, and above all a loyal subject. In fact, Chin sometimes seems to imply that Tu Fu is a great poet precisely because he was a great man. Chin's comments on four lines from the poem "The Trip North" are revealing:

> Though I have gone to register my departure at the palace gate,
> I linger long and apprehensively before leaving it.
> I have indeed fallen short of the standard of a good reminder,
> I fear there might still be something of which His Majesty should
>   be reminded.

And Chin comments, "In the previous section our poet said that he dared not visit home without first being summoned for an audience with the Emperor [to get permission]. In this section he says that he has already been granted an audience, and still he is reluctant to go home. Here we not only see how intricate his style is, but we must also admire its great forcefulness. However, they (*i.e.* the intricacy and the forcefulness) all flow out from an extremely honest heart. Without such an extremely honest heart there cannot be such a forceful and intricate style."[17] Great poetry, so Chin seems to argue, flows only from great hearts.

III *Chin as a Commentator on Tu Fu*

Because the Tu Fu commentary was left unfinished at his death, it is perhaps impossible to discover Chin's total assessment of Tu Fu as a poet; nonetheless, the commentary does provide a basis for examining Chin's own achievement as a commentator. As stated at the beginning of this chapter, in attempting to elucidate Tu Fu's poetic genius, Chin chose to work within a well-established tradition, with a long line of distinguished specialists behind him. It is thus possible to compare his commentary with those of his predecessors', and to see how it differs from others. The publication in 1966 of Professor Yeh Chia-ying's *Tu Fu Ch'iu-hsing pa-shou chi-shuo* (*A Critical Anthology of Commentaries on Tu Fu's "Autumn Thoughts," Eight Poems*) makes such an endeavor easy and convenient. In her anthology, Professor Yeh compares altogether thirty-five different traditional commentaries on the eight poems, including, rather commendably, those of Chin's. We are thus enabled to gain a concentrated view of a group of poems sometimes considered the very best ever written by Tu Fu.[18] For our purpose here we shall not compare Chin with all of the other commentators, but just with those who were ahead of him in time. Before we do, a word should perhaps be said about the poems themselves: their content and the circumstances under which they were composed.

The sequence was written in the autumn of 766, when Tu Fu, already fifty-four years old, was residing temporarily with his family in K'uei-chou, a city by the Yangtze river in present-day eastern Szechwan.[19] The year before (765), with the death of his good friend and patron, Yen Wu, military governor of Chien-nan, Tu Fu and his family had left Ch'eng-tu for a journey down the Yangtze, which they hoped would finally end their exile in Szechwan, and would eventually take them back home to the capital in the north. Their hope, however, was not to be realized. They were detained in K'uei-chou for two full years before they could again sail down the Yangtze. And they were still en route when our poet died in 770.[20]

These eight poems reveal what a prominent position Ch'ang-an, the capital, occupied in Tu Fu's thoughts at this time. Its past glories are contrasted poignantly with the more recent disastrous results of the An Lu-shan Rebellion, which started in 755. Woven skillfully into a panoramic view of the history of the capital city is the sad life story of the poet himself: his brief but glorious days as a court official, his ultimate political failures, and his present hopeless situation as an exile. A sense of loneliness and sadness, but never bitterness, pervades the poems, and these feelings are conveyed in a language whose solitary grandeur and haunting melody are seldom to be seen again in Chinese poetry.

Chin wrote two different commentaries on these poems. According to Chin Ch'ang, editor of a complete collection of Tu Fu commentary, one is incomplete; and Chin Ch'ang rounds it out by adding to it some comments by Hsü Tseng, a close friend of Chin's, whose *Shuo T'ang-shih* (*On T'ang Poetry*) was apparently strongly influenced by Chin.[21] Since Chin Ch'ang failed to indicate which parts belonged to which critic, and instead mixed the comments of Hsü Tseng with those of Chin, our evaluation of Chin as a critic of Tu Fu will necessarily rely more on the second commentary which was presumably written by Chin alone.

Compared with his predecessors, two important features of Chin's commentary stand out immediately. First, his close attention to minute textual details, such as the nuances of words or phrases, the appropriateness of individual words in given contexts, the interrelationships between parts and the whole, etc.[22] Highly interesting new ideas are uncovered as a result. Two or three examples should suffice here. The first couplet in the first poem reads: "Gems of dew wilt and wound the maple trees in the wood:/From Wu mountains, from Wu gorges, the air blows desolate."[23] Most other commentators merely note the desolate atmosphere suggested by these two lines.[24] Chin, too, notes this in his commentary. At the same time, however, he also points out the sharp contrast between the colors "red" and "white" implied in the first line of the couplet: "Dew is called 'gems of dew' (more literally, 'jade dew'), and trees are called 'maple trees.' This is only a scene of desolation, and yet in it the white is made to appear extremely white and the red extremely red. This is why autumn is thought-inducing (*yu-hsing*)."[25] Whether we agree with this conclusion or not, by pointing out the poet's sharply drawn contrast between the colors "white" and "red," which is clearly implied in the first line, Chin adds immensely to our awareness of the poignancy and vividness of a gloomy and desolate scene.

Chin's explication of the first two words in poem four is equally illustrative of his critical habit: "It is said (adapted from Graham's 'well said') Ch'ang-an looks like a chessboard:" "It is said" is a translation of the original *"wen-tao."* What follows in the poem is a description of the changes of the times, the military events that have been besetting the city, and how, like the hibernating fish and dragon in autumn, he can do nothing as an exile but indulge in daydreams about his old home. The question, then, is: Why should Tu Fu choose such an expression (*"wen-tao"*) in this particular context? Other commentators seem unconcerned about this usage as nowhere do they attempt to explain its presence in the line. Chin, with his characteristic habit of hunting down even the most distant nuances, is the sole exception. " 'It is said' is marvelous," he said. "Our poet cannot bear to state things directly, nor does he dare accept rashly [what is reported to have happened]." [26] Chin's point here is clear: what has happened to Ch'ang-an is so sad and shocking that Tu Fu neither has the heart to state the case straightforwardly nor even to believe it. The expression "it is said" tends to create a certain "esthetic distance" between Tu Fu and the poem, and likewise between the reader and the poem. This may seem to be a small point. But a well-chosen diction does constitute the first prerequisite of a good poet. And Chin is particularly good at elucidating poetic diction.

Chin's habit of close scrutiny of the text can also be seen in his awareness of the organic nature of a poem as revealed in subtle changes of meaning in usage. His comments on the first couplet of poem three serve as a good example: "A thousand houses rimmed by the mountains are quiet in the morning light,/Day after day in the house by the river I sit in the blue of the hills." And here are Chin's comments: "After 'a thousand houses rimmed by the mountains' the word 'quiet' is added, then the expression 'morning light.' How graceful (*yu-ch'ü*)! How lovely! 'In the house by the river I sit in the blue of the hills' is also full of incomparable elegance (*chüeh-miao hao-chih*). Yet with the quiet and unobtrusive use of just two characters *'jih-jih'* ('day after day'), the poet has not only cast the river house and the blue hills in a hateful and repugnant light but also made the hilly town and the morning light annoying to the sight." [27] We can only agree with Professor Yeh in saying that "as for what Chin says in the other commentary, it is vivid and clear, and is quite capable of catching the mood and flavor (*ch'ing chih*) of the original." [28]

The second outstanding feature of Chin as a commentator is his inventive spirit, his strong desire to go beyond the obvious for a deeper and fuller understanding of the poem. This accounts for much of the originality of his commentary. His comment on the fifth line of poem one is illustrative: "Clustered chrysanthemums have opened twice, in tears of other days." A word-by-word rendering of the line would be: "Cluster chrysanthemum two open, other day tear." [29] Mr. A. C. Graham, to whom we are indebted for this translation, also provides a detailed analysis of this complex line in the introductory essay ("The Translation of Chinese Poetry") to his *Poems of the Late T'ang*. [30] Most commentators before Chin took the verb "open" in its more obvious meaning as referring to the flowers. Chin, however, thought differently: it is actually the tears, not the flowers, that have burst open: "Those who do not know say that what has opened twice are the clustered chrysanthemums. How could they know that what has opened twice are indeed all the tears of other days?" [31] In other words, while his predecessors all took the word "open" to be an intransitive verb, thus bringing the sentence to an end at the caesura, Chin preferred to take it as a transitive verb which has the "tears of other days" as its object. The question here is not which reading is grammatically more correct, since, as Graham has shown, both are possible. The question is rather which makes for a better poetic reading; which, in other words, realizes more fully the poetic potential of the line. When so viewed, the superiority of Chin's reading stands out readily. Professor Yeh's remark in this regard is worth quoting: "As for Chin's remark in the other commentary that what has opened twice are all the tears of other days . . . it means then that every flower that blossoms becomes a dappled teardrop. . . . What Chin has said is very penetrating and moving." [32]

An even better example of Chin's inventiveness is found in his interpretation of several lines from the middle of the long narrative poem "The Trip North," different from the "Autumn Thoughts" series:

> On top of a slope I gaze at the highlands of Fu-chou,
> At mountain peaks and deep valleys winding in and out.
> I hurry on to the bank of the river,
> My servant is still at the edge of the woods.
> Strange owls hoot among the brown leaves of mulberry trees,
> Field mice peep from scattered holes.
> At midnight we pass a battlefield,
> Where the cold moon shines on the white bones. [33]

The poem is a description of the trip the poet took in 757 from Feng-hsiang to Fu-chou, where his family were then living as refugees. The first four lines present little difficulty. As Chin suggests in his comments, the sight of Fu-chou district, though still some distance away, makes the poet all the more anxious to return home. In his anxiety, he perhaps unconsciously speeds up his horse, so that by the time he has already reached the bottom of a valley, his servant is still dragging behind at the top of a slope far behind him. But what about the second four lines? Our first conclusion would undoubtedly be that they describe a frightfully desolate scene. Chin's interpretation, however, goes much deeper than this. Coming immediately after the previous four lines, he argues, these lines should be taken as a reflection of the inner psychological condition of the poet at that moment. Thus he writes:

The reason why another scenery is described here is this: it has always been that when a man comes home from a thousand *li* away, the hardest part of the journey is after the first nine hundred *li*, when he still has about one hundred *li* to cover before he arrives. His mind will falter . . . and numberless worries and doubts will rush into his head. Now strange owls hoot from the mulberry trees, and field mice peep from scattered holes. What an ominous atmosphere! "Are the members of my family still all alive?" Just in the midst of this great anxiety, he comes upon the white bones on a battlefield under the moonlight late at night. "In nine cases out of ten, they are no longer alive!" These lines are incomparable in describing the anxieties and uncertainties of a traveler about to reach home.[34]

Ironically, Chin's great strength is also his major weakness. While his inventive spirit made him see meanings which his predecessors had failed to see, it also sometimes led him into interpretations unwarranted by the immediate context of the poem. Not infrequently the urge to find deeper hidden meanings became an obsession to be merely different from other commentators, whether his interpretations were justified or not. Reading through his commentary, one cannot help feeling that Chin is occasionally too clever, sometimes to the point of foolishness. This explains the unevenness in his commentary as frequently noted by Professor Yeh in her anthology. For an illustration of this defect of Chin's, however, let us cite two examples not in the "Autumn Thoughts" series.

The first example is a poem entitled "Staying at the Eastern Division One Spring Night" (Ch'un su Tso-sheng):

Flowers disappear under the high wall at dusk;
Twittering birds pass on their way to roost.
Stars twinkle above the ten thousand households;
The moon shines with extra brilliance on the heavenly precincts.
Unable to sleep, I listen for the turning of palace keys,
And the wind reminds me of tinkling jade pendants worn on horses.
I have a memorial to present tomorrow morning.
Several times I wonder how much of the night is past.[35]

The Eastern Division was an annex to the left of the royal palace, where the offices of the Reminders, or Censors, were located. The poem is about a loyal and conscientious official, in this case the poet himself, who is on night duty in the palace and so preoccupied with his responsibilities that he cannot sleep. In the first four lines of the poem, he witnesses stage by stage the process of the deepening of the night: he sees first how the flowers and walls fade into evening colors, how the birds begin to return to their nests, how the stars come out, and, finally, how the moon moves to the center of the sky (midnight). Even then, however, he cannot sleep. Instead, he strains to hear the first sounds of the opening of the palace doors for the morning audience. Even the sound of the wind makes him suspect the approach of high officials riding on horses with jade pendants attached to the reins. The reason for all this fuss is that he has something important to submit to the Emperor in the morning. Several times he wonders about the time, lest he be late for the early court.

In his comments on this poem Chin clearly recognizes that it is about a loyal and conscientious minister suffering a sleepless night. Where he has gone too far, however, is in his reading of lines five and six. He writes: "Line five: 'Unable to sleep, I listen for the turning of palace keys.' Therefore he is thinking that his lord will suffer the misfortune of having his door smashed open. Line six: 'And the wind reminds me of tinkling jade pendants worn on horses.' Therefore he is thinking that among the ministers there will be some who will demonstrate their loyalty by sub-

mitting sound advice instead of bad advice." [36] This poem was
written at a time when the T'ang empire was undergoing a great
upheaval. Two successive large-scale rebellions started by An Lu-
shan and Shih Szu-ming in a period of less than three years
(755–758) shook the empire to its foundation. In 756 the capital
city actually fell into rebel hands, and the royal court had to find
temporary lodging at Ling-wu in the north-west. In commenting
on these two lines, Chin was evidently influenced by the historical
situation, and consequently read into them a meaning unwarranted by the particulars in the poem itself.

A second example of Chin's occasional misreading of a poem is
the frequently quoted "Remembering Li Po on a Spring Day"
(Ch'un-jih huai Li Po):

> Li Po's poetry is unrivaled.
> His soaring thoughts are unique.
> His freshness reminds me of Yü Hsin;
> His delicacy, of Pao Chao.
> Now as I look upon the spring trees north of Wei,
> He is probably watching the evening clouds east of the Chiang.
> When can we meet over a pot of wine,
> Again to study and discuss literature? [37]

Plain and straightforward, the poem expresses Tu Fu's genuine
admiration for Li Po's poetry, and his longing to meet him again
for a convivial discussion of literature and the art of composition
in general. Nothing in the poem itself would call forth a reading
different than this. Chin, however, did not think so. To him, the
poem is rather intended as a friendly admonition to Li Po not to
write freely and carelessly. "Mr. Tu loved Li Po so much," he said,
"that he dared not be the least partial in discussing the art of
writing." [38] In the main body of the commentary, Chin went on to
say: "How can the art of writing be exhausted by such characteri-
zations as 'soaring' and 'unique'? Now when we look at Li Po's
complete works, they show nothing but the qualities of being
'soaring' and 'unique.' This poem not only [served the purpose of]
admonishing Li Po at that time, but will also benefit later writers
a great deal." [39]

Even in his moments of "over-cleverness," however, Chin remains a stimulating commentator. He opens our eyes to new pos-

sibilities, and forces us to think more carefully of what is too often merely taken for granted.

IV *His Personal Style*

The highly personal style which characterizes his *Shui-hu* and *Hsi-hsiang* commentaries is still very much in evidence here. In his Introductory Remarks to a poem called "Leaving Kung-an at Dawn after Having Stayed Here for Several Months" (Hsiao fa Kung-an shu-yueh ch'i-hsi tz'u hsien), for example, he writes: "This poem is 'most vicious' (*tsui o*). I forgot what year it was, but as soon as I saw it, it stuck in my mind. To this day, every dawn on my pillow, when I am about to wake up, but not quite, my mouth would without any reason begin to chant it. In spite of my every effort to stop it, the poem returns repeatedly. Truly my white hair is a gift of this poem." [40] Such was the impact the poem had on him, and his way of expressing the experience is uniquely personal. Similarly, in his comments on another poem, he says, "The sixth month of the summer of the year 1651 was very hot. I read this poem at noon, and I shivered the whole day." [41] Short passages such as these have a way of working themselves into the heart of the reader, and transforming potentially dry and serious discussions into casual, informal conversations, the seriousness of which can be felt nevertheless.

V *Other Commentaries on Traditional Literature*

Besides the Tu Fu commentary, Chin also wrote a number of commentaries on such varied classical texts as the so-called *Nineteen Ancient Poems*,[42] some six hundred Regulated Verse poems of the seven-syllable type by other T'ang writers than Tu Fu, and selected prose works ranging from the *Tso-chuan* to literary essays of the Sung period. In all these commentaries on traditional literature,[43] Chin demonstrates essentially the same characteristics noted above, namely, a close attention to stylistic details and an impulse to be different from other commentators.

CHAPTER 7

His Reputation

I Before 1919 (May Fourth)

EVEN in his own day Chin dazzled his contemporaries with his extraordinary literary talent. Apparently impressed by his clever, sometimes satirical, style of writing, Ch'ien Ch'ien-yi (1582–1664), writing in 1636, claimed that Chin was possessed by a spirit.[1] Obviously apocryphal, the story is nevertheless a good testimonial to the awe in which Chin was held by his contemporaries and the kind of fascination he commanded over them.

From his friends and sympathizers, Chin received nothing but genuine admiration and superlative praise. "Indeed Sheng-t'an is not one," declared Hsü Tseng, a contemporary and friend referred to earlier, "whose range can be detected by those of shallow knowledge and little learning. He was an extraordinary man, very learned, very talented, very superior in knowledge, and very fast with the pen." [2] In his biography of Chin, Liao Yen calls him the first propagator in a thousand years of the merits of authors whose works he had undertaken to annotate, and credits him with the honor of having discovered the entire secret of composition. The anonymous author of the *Hsin-ch'ou chi-wen* eulogizes him in a couplet: "Indulging in wine and engaged in writing was Chin Sheng-t'an,/Whose fame as a genius will not decline in a thousand years." [3] And again, in plain prose: "[The fame of] the seventeen [martyred] people will be handed down to later generations on account of Chin alone." [4]

Being a colorful, controversial individual, naturally Chin did not lack enemies; but almost invariably those who condemned him did so on superficial moral grounds, while totally ignoring the purposes or motives underlying his work and his actual performance as a critic. Among strait-laced critics, his contemporary Kuei Chuang (1613–1673) is representative. In an essay entitled "Exterminating the Devil" (Chu hsieh-kuei), Kuei airs strong disapproval of Chin:

In Soochow there was a man named Chin Sheng-t'an, who was greedy, perverse, licentious, and eccentric, and who did not know the principles of propriety, righteousness, honesty, and shame. Furthermore, he had some literary talent, sufficient to help him in his evil and depraved deeds. He commented on the *Shui-hu chuan* and called it the *Fifth Work of Genius*. It was nicely printed, and widely circulated. When I saw it, I said, "This is a book which advocates disorder." Shortly afterwards, his commentary on the *Hsi-hsiang chi* came out and was known as the *Seventh Work of Genius*.[5] When I saw it, I said, "This is a book which teaches debauchery." Moreover, he took the *Tso-chuan, Shih-chi, Chuang-tzu, Li Sao,* and Tu Fu's poems, put them together with the previous two books, and called them the "Seven Works of Genius." [6] To take fiction and drama, and place them on a par with the Classics, Histroy, Philosophy, and Belles-lettres[7] was in itself already a violation of propriety. On top of this, he deceived the people, corrupted the social customs, and disturbed the scholarly world. His crimes are indeed too numerous to be punished.[8]

At the same time, however, the moralists could not but admit the ever increasing popularity of Chin's critical commentaries among their readers. By the early nineteenth century, the Manchu scholar Chao-lien (1780–1833) reported somewhat grudgingly: "Since Chin Sheng-t'an took delight in annotating the novel [*Shui-hu chuan*], and thought that it both contained all the secret principles of composition and was very similar to Szu-ma Ch'ien's *Shih-chi*, later editions of the novel are without number to the point of being weird, until now there is no scholar's desk on which the *Shui-hu chuan* and *Chin p'ing mei* are not displayed for perusal and amusement." [9]

Concrete evidence of Chin's popularity and influence as a commentator can be seen in the fact that a younger contemporary by the name of Mao Tsung-kang (*fl.* 1661) later undertook to annotate the *San-kuo chih yen-yi* (*Romance of the Three Kingdoms*). In order to assure the popularity of his edition of the novel, Mao forged a preface using Chin's name, in which he praised the novel highly and called it "The First Work of Genius" (*Ti-yi ts'ai-tzu shu*).[10]

II *1919–1949*

The so-called Literary Revolution of the second and third decades of this century represented among other things a reassessment of traditional literary values, including a new awareness of the importance of fiction and drama. Scholars began seriously to devote their time and energy to the study of older popular literary forms. As a result, Chin's position as a pioneer in this field of scholarship came to be fully appreciated and highly praised. While modern scholars may not always share his views or approve his methods, they seldom hesitate to give him credit for his farsightedness in arguing the merits of popular literary masterpieces.

Hu Shih, a leader of the Literary Revolution, helped to set the tone when, in his "*Shui-hu chuan* k'ao cheng" ("A Textual Study of the *Shui-hu chuan*"), he called Chin "a great uncanny genius" (*ta kuai chieh*) endowed with extraordinary critical insight and great intellectual audacity.[11] In his preface to the 120-chapter edition of the *Shui-hu chuan,* he praises him by saying: "Sheng-t'an's ability to debate was invincible; his pen was most persuasive. During his time, he had the reputation of a genius. His death was also a case of extreme cruelty, which shook the whole country. After his death, his reputation became even greater. In the field of fiction criticism, his power and prestige completely overshadowed those of other well-known critics such as Wang Shih-chen (1526–1590), Li Chih (1527–1602), Chung Hsing (1574–1624), etc. . . ."[12] Moreover, Hu praised Chin in spite of his dislike of Chin's methodology, which he calls "mechanical" (*chi-hsieh*) and "smacking of the compiler of eight-legged essays" (*yu pa-ku hsüan-chia ch'i*).[13] Liu Fu (1891–1934), another participant in the Literary Revolution, records his excitement over the discovery of Chin's original edition of the *Shui-hu chuan* in his own preface to a photolithographic edition of the same work, and calls Chin's the best edition as far as literary value is concerned. In the same preface he also praises Chin as a great benefactor of the *Shui-hu chuan*.[14] We have already seen at the end of Chapter 4 how Chou Tso-jen observed that he liked Chin's comments as much as he liked the *Shui-hu chuan* itself. Probably for the same reason, Lin Yutang termed Chin "that great impressionistic critic of the seventeenth century"[15] and took pains to render into English a number of passages from Chin's commentaries. Even Lu Hsün, who ob-

jected to Chin's truncation of the novel, and who seems to have
cared little for Chin's personality as it emerges from his writings,[16]
had to grant that his edition of the *Shui-hu chuan* is not without
its stylistic attractions.[17]

III   *Since 1949*

Just when Chin's standing as a farsighted and uniquely talented
critic seemed to be gaining general acceptance, a different interpretation began to take shape in China. Following the change in
government on the Chinese mainland in 1949, a broad and wide-
ranging reevaluation of the past was sponsored by the new government. The *Shui-hu chuan* is still hailed as one of the greatest
novels China has ever produced; it is praised, however, not only
for its artistic achievement, but also for its masterful portrayal of
"peasant resistance to the ruling class." [18] Similarly, the *Hsi-hsiang
chi* also attains a socio-political significance: it is taken to repre-
sent an open revolt on the part of the young against an old, out-
moded marriage system.[19] As has been noted earlier, although
sympathetic toward the individual heroes (except Sung Chiang)
in the *Shui-hu chuan*, Chin was unrelenting in his condemnation
of them as outlaws who dared to defy orders from the court. In
the case of the *Hsi-hsiang chi*, he remodeled the character of Ying-
ying in such a way as to make her actions appear more consistent
with those of a well-bred young lady. In both these respects, then,
his views were bound to conflict with Marxist critical opinion.
Therefore, he is today criticized, attacked, and categorically condemned. Of the many attacks on Chin, the longest and most ambitious is Ho Man-tzu's *Lun Chin Sheng-t'an p'ing kai Shui-hu
chuan* (*On Chin Sheng-t'an's Critique and Revision of the
Shui-hu chuan*). It thus deserves close examination.

Although the book is ostensibly an evaluation of Chin's commentary on the *Shui-hu chuan*, almost two-thirds of the total is
devoted to discussions of Chin's philosophy of life and literary
theory in general. Of the nine chapters in the book, only the last
three are concerned with Chin's criticism of the novel. Chin is
variously called "another kind of spokesman for the feudal, ruling
class" (*feng-chien t'ung-chih chieh-chi ti yu yi-chung tai-yen-jen*)
(Chapter 2), "a fatalistic nihilist" (*su-ming-kuan ti hsü-wu chu-yi
che*) (Chapter 3), "A sophist" (*kuei-pien-lun che*) (Chapter 4),
"a jester of life" (*p'iao-yu jen-sheng*) (Chapter 5), and "a formal-

ist" (*hsing-shih chu-yi che*) in art theory (Chapter 6). Chin's contributions to the appreciation of the *Shui-hu chuan* are totally ignored, while all the "evil" and "wicked" things he did to the novel by way of emendation are carefully catalogued (Chapters 7–9). The end result is a picture distorted out of all proportion to reality.

More recently, however, a more balanced view of the subject has been advanced on the Chinese mainland, and by a literary historian no less eminent than Liu Ta-chieh. In an article entitled "The Literary Criticism of Chin Sheng-t'an" (Chin Sheng-t'an ti wen-hsüeh p'i-p'ing),[20] Liu and his collaborator Chang P'ei-heng, while calling attention to backward and "feudalistic" elements in Chin's political thought, at the same time point out the significant contribution of Chin as a literary critic. In much the same way, Chu Chao-nien has reached similar conclusions in an article on "How to Evaluate the Literary Theory of Chin Jen-jui: An Examination of His Commentary on the *Hsi-hsiang chi*" (Tsen-yang p'ing-chia Chin Jen-jui ti wen-hsüeh li-lun—chien t'an Chin-p'i *Hsi-hsiang chi*).[21] By thus separating literary criticism from politics, Chin's achievements as a literary critic have once more been approached and examined in an objective and disinterested way.

This is in brief the history of Chin's reputation as a literary critic over the past three centuries. With the exception of the post-1949 period, it can be said that he has not done badly. His commentaries on the *Shui-hu chuan* and *Hsi-hsiang chi* have been particularly well received. In fact, they have been so well received that for a long time his editions of the two works have enjoyed the widest popularity. His *Shui-hu chuan* fared even better, as Irwin remarked in his study of the novel, ". . . his (*i.e.* Chin's) edition of the novel found such an enthusiastic reception that throughout the entire Ch'ing dynasty, . . . the very existence of its predecessors was virtually forgotten." [22]

In summation, Chin's contributions to Chinese literary history can be said to have been twofold: he was one of the earliest and most influential promoters of vernacular literature, and, secondly, he developed a productive method of literary analysis that placed its emphasis on close textual examination. Whereas the first contribution is largely historical, the second one is more intrinsic, and hence more permanent and valuable. As a critic, Chin has his limitations, even serious limitations, as we have pointed out throughout this study. But we must not be so distracted by his faults as to lose sight of his true merits. All things considered, Chin has to be ranked as one of the most original literary critics in Chinese history. In the field of fiction criticism especially, he is peerless.

Notes and References

The romanization system used throughout is the Wade-Giles with modifications: 1) all diacritical marks are omitted except in cases where they are essential, and where they are needed to facilitate pronunciation; 2) when "*i*" alone is used to stand for a syllable, it is invariably changed to "*yi.*"

Names of authors (sometimes titles when authorship is unknown) that are also cited in the appended Bibliography appear in capital letters. Chinese titles in this Notes section are usually followed by an English translation, except for those titles which are cited in the Bibliography, where all titles are translated. Similarly, publication information is omitted for those titles that are to appear again in the Bibliography.

References to older Chinese texts (or a modern reprint or resetting of an older text) are represented by two sets of numerals separated by a virgule, with the one to the left indicating the *chüan* ("volume") number and the one to the right the page number. When letters "a" and "b" appear with the numeral or numerals to the right of the virgule, they refer to *recto* and *verso* respectively.

Chapter One

1. René Wellek and Austin Warren in their *Theory of Literature* (New York, 1956, p. 201), for example, think that the inferiority of fiction criticism in both quantity and quality is due to the lack of serious regard scholars have traditionally shown toward narrative fiction.

2. See JAMES J. Y. LIU, *The Art of Chinese Poetry* (hereafter, James Liu), Part II, 1, esp. pp. 65–66.

3. For examples, see Wang Hsiao-ch'uan (comp.), *Yuan Ming Ch'ing san-tai chin hui hsiao-shuo hsi-ch'ü shih-liao* (*Source Materials on the Banning and Destruction of Fiction and Drama during the Three Dynasties of Yuan, Ming, and Ch'ing*) (Peking, 1958.)

4. *Cf.* CHOU TSO-JEN, *Chung-kuo hsin-wen-hsüeh ti yuan-liu,* esp. pp. 36, 43, 52–53, 57.

5. For a more detailed account of the Antiquarian Movement and the Kung-an School, see KUO SHAO-YÜ, *Chung-kuo wen-hsüeh*

p'i-p'ing shih, vol. 2, pp. 171–283. A less detailed, but more concise, account can be found in LIU TA-CHIEH, *Chung-kuo wen-hsüeh fa-ta shih,* pp. 849–64. The literary views of the Antiquarians are also succinctly discussed in James Liu, Part II, 3, esp. pp. 78–80. See also ANDRÉ LÉVY, "Un Document sur la Querelle des Anciens et des Modernes More Sinico."

6. See biography of Li Meng-yang in *Ming-shih* (*History of Ming*), *chüan* 286 (K'ai-ming Bookstore *Er-shih-wu shih* ed., 1935, vol. 9, p. 708b).

7. "A Letter in Reply to Mr. Chou" (Ta Chou-tzu shu) in *K'ung-t'ung chi* (*Collected Works of* [*Li*] *K'ung-t'ung*), undated woodblock edition in the Hoover Library of Stanford University, 62/13a–b. English translation cited from James Liu, p. 80.

8. See Jung Chao-tsu, *Li Cho-wu p'ing-chuan* (*A Critical Biography of Li Cho-wu*) (Shanghai, 1937), esp. pp. 69–100; Hsiao Kung-ch'üan, "Li Chih: An Iconoclast of the Sixteenth Century", *T'ien Hsia Monthly,* 6:4 (April, 1938), pp. 317–41; and Wm. Theodore de Bary, "Individualism and Humanitarianism in Late Ming Thought," in *Self and Society in Ming Thought,* edited by Wm. Theodore de Bary (New York, 1970), pp. 145–247, esp. pp. 193–97.

9. "T'ung-hsin shuo" ("On the Mind of the Child") in his *Fen-shu* (*A Book to Burn*) (Peking, 1961 ed.), p. 110.

10. *Ibid.,* p. 111.

11. *Ibid.*

12. *Ku* is short for *ku-shih* or *ku-t'i-shih,* a type of verse that came into being during the Han Dynasty (206 B.C.–220 A.D.). *Hsüan* stands for *hsüan-t'i-shih,* which refers to the poems collected in the sixth century anthology *Wen-hsüan.* Since all the *shih* poems in the *Wen-hsüan* are of the *ku-shih* type, the term *hsüan-t'i-shih* is sometimes also used to mean *ku-shih* in general. See James Liu, pp. 24–26, for a description of the prosodic features of the Ancient Verse.

13. A term used in contrast to the Ancient Verse, it refers specifically to the *lü-shih* (Regulated Verse) and the *chüeh-chü* (Quatrain) types of verse that flourished during the T'ang Dynasty (618–907). See James Liu, pp. 26–29, for a description of their prosodic features.

14. Short stories written in the literary language during the T'ang period.

15. A type of theatrical performance known to have flourished during the Chin dynasty (twelfth century).

16. Yuan dynasty drama of the northern type, in which the *Hsi-hsiang chi* was written.

17. A type of short essay in eight parts officially standardized in the 1480s as the only type allowed in the traditional civil service

examinations. Ch'en Shou-yi in his *Chinese Literature: A Historical Introduction* (New York, 1961), pp. 501–509, discusses this type of essay at some length.

18. In *Fen-shu,* p. 111.

19. See, for example, his "Wen-hsüeh kai-liang ch'u-yi" ("Some Rough Suggestions for a Literary Reform") and "Li-shih ti wen-hsüeh kuan-nien lun" ("Literature in Historical Perspective") in HU SHIH, *Hu Shih wen-ts'un,* vol. 1, pp. 5–17 and 33–36 respectively, esp. pp. 7, 33.

20. "Evolution" is a key term frequently used by Hu Shih in his article "Wen-hsüeh kai-liang ch'u-yi," mentioned in the previous note.

21. *Op. cit.,* pp. 863–64.

22. See RICHARD G. IRWIN, *The Evolution of a Chinese Novel,* p. 108, note 25.

23. *Yuan Chung-lang shih-chi* (*The Poetical Works of Yuan Chung-lang*), p. 185, in *Yuan Chung-lang ch'üan-chi* (Complete Works) (Taipei, 1964 ed.). Lung-hu was Li Chih's style.

24. "Hsüeh-t'ao ko chi hsü" ("Preface to the Collections of Hsüeh-t'ao ko", *i.e.* Chiang Ying-k'o), *Yuan Chung-lang wen-ch'ao* (*The Prose Works of Yuan Chung-lang*), p. 6, in *Yuan Chung-lang ch'üan-chi* (*q.v.*).

25. *Ibid.,* p. 7.

26. "Hua yun fu yin" ("Preface to the *Fu* on Flowers and Clouds") by Chou Sheng-k'ai, in *K'o-hsüeh chai chi* (*Collected Prose Works of K'o-hsüeh chai, i.e.* Yuan Chung-tao) (Shanghai, 1936 ed.), p. 32.

27. "Lun wen" ("On Writing") in *Po-Su chai lei-chi* (*Collected Works of Po-Su chai, i.e.* Yuan Tsung-tao) (Shanghai, 1935 ed.), p. 253.

28. *Yuan Chung-lang wen-ch'ao* (*The Prose Works of Yuan Chung-lang*), *q.v.,* p. 5.

29. *Ibid.,* p. 6. *Cf.* tr. by Ch'en Shou-yi, *op. cit.,* p. 514.

30. A section in the *Shih-chi.*

31. *Yuan Chung-lang shih-chi* (*The Poetical Works of Yuan Chung-lang*), *q.v.,* p. 21.

32. The various *Shui-hu* commentaries attributed to Li Chih may all be spurious (see HU SHIH, *Hu Shih wen-ts'un,* vol. 3, p. 421). In any case, they (the so-called Jung-yü t'ang ed., for example) are usually brief, and are not very helpful in the elucidation of the work's literary characteristics.

33. *T'ang ts'ai-tzu shih* (*Poems by Geniuses of T'ang*) (hereafter, *T'ang Poetry Commentary*), 5/297.

34. First Preface to the *Kuan-hua t'ang yuan-pen Shui-hu chuan: Ti-wu ts'ai-tzu shu* (*Kuan-hua Study's Original Edition of the Shui-hu chuan: The Fifth Work of Genius*) (hereafter, *Shui-hu Commen-*

tary), vol. 1, 1/9b. Shih Nai-an was the putative author of the *Shui-hu chuan,* while Tung Chieh-yuan (Scholar Tung), who lived during the Chin (twelfth century), wrote what was to become the immediate forerunner of Wang Shih-fu's *Hsi-hsiang chi,* which was considered by Chin to be one of the *Six Works of Genius.*

35. *Hsien-ch'ing ou-chi,* pp. 65–66.

Chapter Two

1. In his *Er-shih-ch'i sung-t'ang chi,* 6/5a-6a. (Hereafter, Liao Yen.)

2. In its account of Chin and the circumstances of his death, it is almost identical with the *K'U-MIAO CHI-LÜEH.*

3. A good example is the confusion concerning his name, which is discussed in full in note 7 below. YANG KUNG-TAO's *Chin Sheng-t'an yi-shih* collects many stories and legends about Chin.

4. Hereafter, Ch'en Teng-yuan.

5. Hereafter, Fang.

6. Pp. 87–94. (Hereafter, Irwin.)

7. There has been a great deal of confusion with regard to his name. According to the *K'U-MIAO CHI-LÜEH* and *HSIN-CH'OU CHI-WEN,* Chin's original family name was Chang, his personal name Ts'ai (sometimes also known as K'uei), and his *tzu* Jo-ts'ai. It is said that in the examination for the *hsiu-ts'ai* degree (the first of the three degrees in the old civil service examination system), he wrote an essay so exotic and wild (*kuai tan*) that he was failed, and that in order to sit again he changed his family name to Chin and personal name to Jen-jui. On this second try, he produced an orthodox paper of such high standard that he gained first place. Liao Yen, however, tells the story differently. According to him, Chin's personal name was Ts'ai, and his *tzu* K'u-ts'ai (which could be a misprint for Jo-ts'ai). Liao says that after the change of dynasty in 1644 (and not because of the official examination), Chin changed his personal name to Jen-jui, and his *tzu* to Sheng-t'an. But Liao doesn't say that Chin's family name was also changed; nor does he mention Chin's spectacular performance in the examination.

That Chin changed his personal name and *tzu* seems possible, since all the available accounts refer to this fact regardless of the specific circumstances cited. Ch'en Teng-yuan (pp. 2–5) has argued rather convincingly against the belief that he changed his family name, the most important evidence supporting his argument being the fact that Chin had a third cousin on the paternal side with the name of Chin Ch'ang who was responsible for collecting many of Chin's manuscripts for publication after his death. The confusion about his family name may also have arisen from the fact that there was some one by the name of Chang Jo-ts'ai who lived not far from Soochow, Chin's home town. (See Ch'en Teng-yuan, p. 3; *cf.* Fang, p. 164.)

8. Karashima, pp. 539–42; Ch'en Teng-yuan, pp. 7–8.

9. Fang Chao-ying and Richard Irwin, for example.

10. *Shui-hu Commentary*, vol. 1, Preface 3, 1/16b.

11. See below, note 24.

12. See *Shui-hu Commentary*, vol. 1, Preface 3, 1/16a.

13. *Ibid.*, vol. 18, 53/18a.

14. *Hui-t'u Hsi-hsiang chi: Ti-liu ts'ai-tzu shu* (*Illustrated Hsi-hsiang chi: The Sixth Work of Genius*) (hereafter, *Hsi-hsiang Commentary*), 2/2a–b (No. 14). These probably formed the basis of a much larger collection posthumously printed as the *Ts'ai-tzu pi-tu shu* (*Required Works for Geniuses*).

15. "Ts'ai-tzu shu hsiao-yin" ("Foreword to the Works of Genius") in *Kuan-hua t'ang ts'ai-tzu shu hui-kao* (*Collected Works of Genius of the Kuan-hua Study*) (hereafter *Collected Works*), vol. 1.

16. *Shui-hu Commentary*, vol. 1, Preface 3, 1/16a–b.

17. XII:20.

18. See *Hsi-hsiang Commentary*, 5/6b.

19. *Shui-hu Commentary*, vol. 20, 61/3b–4a.

20. *Hsi-hsiang Commentary*, 4/18b.

21. For what follows in this paragraph, see *Shui-hu Commentary*, vol. 1, 1/16b–17a, 19b (Preface 3).

22. *Tu-shih chieh* (*Analysis of Tu Fu's Poetry*) in *Collected Works*, vols. 1–3, 3/19b; hereafter, *Tu Fu Commentary*.

23. *Ibid.*

24. All the extant records indicate that Chin was a holder of the *hsiu-ts'ai* degree, but none of them specify when he actually took the degree. Judging from the fact that he did not start his schooling until his ninth year, and in view of the long and arduous preparations required for the examinations, I have tentatively placed the date in his late teens.

25. According to CHOU TSO-JEN, the printing of this collection was probably never quite completed. This is why no copy of it is to be seen anywhere today. See his article "T'an Chin Sheng-t'an," p. 14. For the eight-legged essay, see note 17, Chap. 1.

26. The list of the thirty-three delights is found in the *Hsi-hsiang Commentary*, 7/7b–9b. LIN YUTANG has made a complete translation of the list in his *The Importance of Living*, pp. 131–36. The following selections are translated in consultation with Lin's translation. The assignment of the date to Chin's late twenties has been arrived at this way: Chin's *Hsi-hsiang* commentary was supposedly completed in 1656 (see below, p. 33), and Chin states in his com-

ments that the enumeration of these delights actually took place some twenty years earlier. Assuming Chin was born in 1610, this would place the date somewhere around his twenty-sixth year.

27. As LIAO YEN states in his biography of Chin (6/5a), Wang Cho-shan was Chin's best friend. Numerous affectionate and highly complimentary references are made to Wang in Chin's commentaries to both the *Shui-hu* and the *Hsi-hsiang* (some of the references are assembled in Ch'en Teng-yuan, pp. 21–23). In fact, Chin and Wang regarded each other as brothers and shared the same basic views on life (*Hsi-hsiang Commentary*, 6/9a).

28. Cited in Ch'en Teng-yuan, p. 29, and CHOU TSO-JEN, "T'an Chin Sheng-t'an", pp. 12–13. I have had the chance to examine only three different editions of this work, but none of them contains this preface by Hsü Tseng.

29. *Tu Fu Commentary*, 3/22a.

30. Liao Yen, 6/5a. Kuan-hua Study was actually the name of his friend Han Chu's study, where he found a so-called "old text" of the *Shui-hu chuan* (see p. 26, above). Since Chin called his version of the *Shui-hu chuan* the *Kuan-hua t'ang yuan-pen Shui-hu chuan*, some later writers (LIAO YEN included) have inadvertently taken Kuan-hua Study to have been Chin's own. For a further discussion of this problem, see Ch'en Teng-yuan, pp. 24–25.

31. *Shui-hu Commentary*, vol. 5, 17/3a.

32. See below, Chap. 4, Section III.

33. *Shui-hu Commentary*, vol. 1, Preface 2, 1/13b.

34. See below, Chap. 4, Section III.

35. See *ibid.*

36. *Shui-hu Commentary*, vol. 1, Preface 3, 1/19b.

37. *Ibid.*, vol. 24, 75/1a.

38. That the preface is a forgery has since been proved by Hu Shih and other scholars. See Irwin, p. 91, for a further discussion of this problem.

39. *Shui-hu Commentary*, vol. 6, 19/1b.

40. The "Yang Chu Chapter" translated in Wm. Theodore de Bary (ed.), *Sources of Chinese Tradition* (New York, 1960), pp. 290–291.

41. *Shui-hu Commentary*, vol. 6, 19/1b–2a.

42. *Ibid.*, vol. 5, 18/3a.

43. *Ibid.*, vol. 12, 36/1b.

44. LIN YUTANG has translated the entire preface into English in his *The Importance of Understanding*, pp. 83–85. Pearl Buck's translation can be found in her translation of the novel *All Men Are Brothers* (London, 1937), vol. 1, pp. xii–xiv.

45. Liao Yen, 6/5a.

46. *T'ang Poetry Commentary*, p. 539.

47. *Hsi-hsiang Commentary*, 5/9b. Contained in the Introductory Remarks to Part II, Act II, part of which is translated by LIN YU-TANG in his *The Importance of Living*, pp. 334–38.

48. *Hsi-hsiang Commentary*, 5/15a.

49. See below, Chap. 5, Section III.

50. 7/22a.

51. They were T'ien-tsai, Chuang-yen, Chan-t'an, An-hsiang, Chieh-t'o, Tun-hou, Yun-tsai, and K'ai-yun. The correspondence can be found in the *T'ang Poetry Commentary*, pp. 582, 583, and 585 respectively.

52. This information is provided by Chin himself in his preface to the *T'ang Poetry Commentary*, 1/1.

53. Chin himself said 600.

54. *HSIN-CH'OU CHI-WEN* put it in between the years 1659 and 1660.

55. "Hsü *Ti-szu ts'ai-tzu shu*" ("Preface to the *Fourth Work of Genius*") in *Collected Works*, vol. 1.

56. The account of this incident is based mainly upon the *K'U-MIAO CHI-LÜEH*.

57. *K'U-MIAO CHI-LÜEH*, p. 2a.

58. *Ibid.*, pp. 2b–3a.

59. *Ibid.*, p. 8b.

60. *Ibid.*, p. 9a.

61. See, for example, Ch'en Teng-yuan, pp. 32–37; and Fang, p. 164.

62. Most Chinese Communist authors hold this view. By far the most ambitious and articulate attack on Chin is to be found in HO MAN-TZU's *Lun Chin Sheng-t'an p'ing kai Shui-hu chuan*. For a discussion of this book and other major Marxist interpretations of Chin, see Chap. 7, Section III below.

63. See below, Chap. 4, end of Section III, for a further discussion of this point.

64. In *Collected Works*, vol. 5, "Sui-shou t'ung" ("Casual Jottings"), p. 7b. Note the echo of the *Great Learning*.

65. *Tu Fu Commentary*, 1/23a. *Cf.* below, p. 111.

66. *Analects*, XVII:9.

67. *Shui-hu Commentary*, vol. 2, 7/2b.

68. *I.e.* Yen Hui, Confucius's favorite disciple noted for conduct.

69. Liao Yen, 6/5a–b. Tseng Tien, whose personal name was Hsi, was another disciple of Confucius. According to the *Analects* (XI:25), Confucius was one day sitting with four disciples. When asked to state their ambitions in life, three of them expressed a desire to work in government. When Tseng Tien's turn came, he put down the lute

he had been strumming all the time, and replied, "In late spring, when the spring clothes are made, I would like with five or six adults and six or seven boys to bathe in the river Yi, cool ourselves in the breeze among the rain altars and return home singing." Whereupon Confucius, sighing deeply, said, "I am with Tien."

Chapter Three

1. *The Mirror and the Lamp* (hereafter, Abrams), p. 3. The words in parentheses have been added.

2. *Ibid.*, pp. 21–22.

3. *Ibid.*, p. 23.

4. *Ibid.*, p. 3.

5. *Shang-shu t'ung-chien* (Peking, 1936), 02/0681–0683.

6. For the controversy over the meaning of the character *chih*, see James Liu, pp. 72–73.

7. Translation from James Liu, p. 70.

8. *T'ang Poetry Commentary*, pp. 545–46. Translation from James Liu, p. 73.

9. *Tu Fu Commentary*, 3/9b.

10. *Ibid.*, 3/9b–10a.

11. *Cf.* Abrams, p. 154.

12. *T'ang Poetry Commentary*, p. 546. Translation from James Liu, p. 74.

13. *Ibid.*, p. 544.

14. *Ibid.*, pp. 544–45. Ts'ang Ti is Ts'ang Chieh, to whom is attributed the invention of Chinese characters.

15. *Ibid.*, p. 577.

16. Abrams, p. 26.

17. Both quoted in Abrams, p. 26.

18. *T'ang Poetry Commentary*, p. 560. Translation from James Liu, p. 75.

19. *Tu Fu Commentary*, 1/12a. Translations of the terms *"wen jou tun hou"* are patterned after James Liu, p. 67, who also gives a brief exposition of Shen Te-ch'ien's poetic theory.

20. See Abrams, Chapters VII and VIII.

21. See Burton Watson (tr.), *The Complete Works of Chuang Tzu* (New York, 1968), pp. 50–51 and 152–53 respectively.

22. Trans. by Prof. Shih-hsiang Chen in Cyril Birch (ed.), *Anthology of Chinese Literature* (New York, 1965), p. 213.

23. Translation from Vincent Yu-chung Shih (tr.), *The Literary Mind and the Carving of Dragons* (New York, 1959), p. 154.

24. *Hsi-hsiang Commentary*, 2/2b–3a (No. 18).

25. *Ibid.*, 2/3a (No. 21).

26. *Ibid.*, 2/3b (No. 22).

27. *Cf.* below, Chap. 4, Section IV A.

28. *Shui-hu Commentary*, vol. 1, 1/18a (Preface 3).

29. These two terms occur in the *Analects*, IV:5. For a discussion of their place in the Confucian system of ideas, see Fung Yu-lan, *A Short History of Chinese Philosophy* (New York, 1962), pp. 43–44.

30. *Shui-hu Commentary*, vol. 1, 1/18a (Preface 3). "Ten years" is just a round number, which does not necessarily have a historical basis. The language of this passage of course echoes the *Great Learning*.

31. *Ibid.*, 1/18b. This is a typical example of Chin's eclecticism. While the use of the concept *yuan* (cause) to account for the existence of things in the world is distinctly Buddhist, the idea of *ko wu* (investigation of things) is thoroughly Neo-Confucian.

32. *Ibid.*, 1/19b.

33. *Ibid.*, vol. 20, 60/1b–2a.

34. *Ibid.*, 60/2a–b.

35. Contained in M. H. Abrams (ed.), *The Norton Anthology of English Literature* (New York, 1962), vol. 2, pp. 405–406.

36. *Shui-hu Commentary*, vol. 1, 5/3a.

37. *Ibid.*, 1/12a (Preface 1).

38. *T'ang Poetry Commentary*, p. 557.

39. *Shui-hu Commentary*, vol. 1, 1/20b, (Preface 3).

40. 4/17a.

41. See note 18, Chapter 1.

42. *Shui-hu Commentary*, vol. 1, 5/3b.

43. *Hsi-hsiang Commentary*, 2/1b (No. 8).

44. Vol. 1, 1/22b–23a.

45. 2/3b. Tr. in consultation w. Ch'en Shou-yi, *op. cit.*, p. 563.

46. *Ts'ang-lang shih-hua chiao shih* (*Discussions of Poetry by Ts'ang-lang Collated and Annotated* [by Kuo Shao-yü]) (Peking, 1962), p. 142.

47. *Ibid.*, p. 155.

48. M. H. Abrams, *A Glossary of Literary Terms* (New York, 1964), p. 22.

49. *Hsi-hsiang Commentary*, 2/1b (No. 9).

50. *Shui-hu Commentary*, vol. 1, 1/21a (Preface 3).

51. *Ibid.*, vol. 1, 3/2b.

Chapter Four

1. IRWIN has a résumé of the entire novel, chapter by chapter, in his *The Evolution of a Chinese Novel*, pp. 117–201.

2. Irwin, pp. 89–94, discusses briefly Chin's motives and methods

as editor. See also James J. Y. Liu, *The Chinese Knight-Errant* (Chicago, 1967), pp. 110–111.

3. The publication of the *Shui-hu ch'üan-chuan* (The Complete *Shui-hu chuan*), a variorum edition in four volumes compiled under the editorship of Cheng Chen-to and others and published by Jen-min wen-hsüeh ch'u-pan-she, 1954, makes the checking of Chin's textual changes an easy task. Based mainly on the T'ien-tu wai-ch'en (Wang Tao-k'un) edition of 1589, it also painstakingly records variant readings from eight other editions, including Chin's edition. The so-called "older edition" used to check Chin's version of the novel in this chapter refers to this variorum edition. HO HSIN in his *Shui-hu yen-chiu* (hereafter, Ho Hsin) also devotes a complete chapter (6) to a discussion of Chin's revisions.

4. For a translation of *"hsieh-tzu"* ("peg") as "Induction," see James J. Y. Liu, *Elizabethan and Yuan* (London, 1955), pp. 10–11.

5. Irwin himself (p. 51) is inclined to view the novel as the joint work of Shih Nai-an and Lo Kuan-chung. See also Liu, *The Chinese Knight-Errant*, pp. 108–110.

6. Vol. 1, p. 360.

7. See Ho Hsin, p. 127. Ho Hsin has compiled a chronology for the novel.

8. See Ho Hsin, p. 128.

9. The use of verse in prose narratives has been traced by many scholars to the so-called *pien-wen* of the ninth and tenth centuries. *Pien-wen* is considered the forerunner of traditional Chinese vernacular fiction. It is a mixed genre of verse and prose, in which verse occasionally is used to advance the narrative as well as to recapitulate or comment on the prose tale. It has been noted that as time went on, verse gradually ceased to function as an integral part of the narrative, until it became, as in later vernacular novels and short stories, a mere convention whose function is more decorative than structural. For a summary discussion of the meaning of the term *pien-wen*, see Liu, *The Chinese Knight-Errant*, p. 210, note 9.

10. *Cf.* C. T. HSIA, *The Classic Chinese Novel*, p. 100.

11. Vol. 1, p. 407. King Yu (reigned B.C. 781–770) was the last king of Western Chou. His downfall was often associated with his infatuation with the beautiful but wicked Lady Pao-szu. "Dragon Spring" is the name of a famous sword in ancient China. The English translation throughout this chapter, unless otherwise noted, is mine.

12. Vol. 1, p. 345.

13. Vol. 8, 27/14b.

14. Vol. 1, p. 102.

15. Vol. 3, 10/22b–23a.

16. This is the English version of his *Chung-kuo hsiao-shuo shih-*

lüeh. The example is quoted below in Section IV C under Technique 2.

17. Vol. 1, p. 417.

18. Vol. 10, 30/26a-b. See also Ho Hsin, p. 117.

19. Vol. 23, 68/15b. *Cf.* Ho Hsin, pp. 109–111.

20. Irwin, p. 91.

21. Jaroslav Prušek, "Boccaccio and His Chinese Contemporaries," *New Orient* 7:2 (April, 1968), 45–48; and 7:3 (June, 1968), 65–68. The above quotations appear on p. 68.

22. Irwin, p. 91.

23. "T'an Chin Sheng-t'an," *Lu Hsün ch'üan-chi,* vol. 4, p. 404.

24. See note 3 above.

25. This essay is included as an appendix to his *A Brief History of Chinese Fiction,* p. 419.

26. Vol. 2, 6/1a–b.

27. Vol. 19, 56/2a–b.

28. Vol. 19, 56/11a.

29. Vol. 5, 15/9a.

30. Vol. 14, 43/22a.

31. Vol. 10, 32/1b.

32. See above, Chap. 2, p. 30.

33. Vol. 1, 1/13a–b.

34. Vol. 1, 3/1b–2a.

35. CHANG YU-LUAN in his article "Chin Sheng-t'an tsen-yang wu-mieh Sung Chiang ti" has made a full investigation of this aspect of Chin's commentary. See also Ho Hsin, pp. 120–123.

36. Vol. 7, 22/1a–b.

37. See below, Section IV C, Technique 5, for more examples.

38. In Chapter 64 of Chin's version, for example, upon hearing the name Liang-shan-p'o, an old man is made to say, "That Chief Sung on the mountain doesn't rob people traveling by, nor does he kill people. He only carries out Heaven's Way." Later, this same old man again remarks, "I have heard that Sung Chiang and his group are truly humane and righteous. They rescue the poor and help the old. . . ." (Vol. 23, 69/12a–b.)

39. Vol. 1, 2/6b–7b.

40. Vol. 24, 75/22b.

41. Vol. 24, 75/23a.

42. *"Shui-hu chuan* k'ao-cheng," *Hu Shih wen-ts'un,* vol. 1, p. 545.

43. CHAO TS'UNG, *Chung-kuo szu ta hsiao-shuo chih yen-chiu,* p. 27.

44. The whole decree bearing this date is contained in Wang Hsiao-ch'uan (comp.), *Yüan Ming Ch'ing san-tai chin hui hsiao-shuo hsi-ch'ü shih-liao (Source Materials on the Banning and Destruction*

of Fiction and Drama during the Three Dynasties of Yuan, Ming and Ch'ing) (Peking, 1958), p. 15.

45. *Cf.* LIU TA-CHIEH and CHANG P'EI-HENG, "Chin Sheng-t'an ti wen-hsüeh p'i-p'ing."

46. *Collected Works,* 1/10a.

47. *Ibid.,* 2/11b. This identification of Heaven with the people contains an obvious reference to the *Mencius* (Va:5).

48. *Ibid.,* 1/10a.

49. Vol. 2, 7/2a.

50. *Hsi-hsiang Commentary,* 5/19b.

51. *Shui-hu Commentary,* vol. 24, 75/2a–b.

52. Vol. 1, 1/22a–b. Yi-hsiang was a historian of the Ch'u state during the Spring and Autumn period.

53. *Shui-hu Commentary,* vol. 1, 1/17b.

54. *Ibid.,* 1/21b.

55. *Ibid.,* 3/3a.

56. *Ibid.,* 3/3b.

57. Vol. 1, 1/18a. See above, Chap. 3, Section II, for further discussion by Chin on this matter.

58. Vol. 1, 3/5a.

59. Vol. 1, 3/6b–7a.

60. Vol. 1, 3/5a.

61. Vol. 8, 27/15b–16a. Section V below contains a full translation of Wu Sung's fight with the tiger, accompanied by Chin's comments.

62. Vol. 1, 3/11a. Chin is here addressing his own son, for whom the commentary is meant. Hence, the expression "young people of other families."

63. The fifteen techniques are enumerated in that section of his commentary (vol. 1, 3/11a–15b) called "How to Read the *Fifth Work of Genius.*" In *The Evolution of a Chinese Novel* (p. 93), Mr. Irwin translated partially six of these techniques (Nos. 3, 5, 6, 8, 9, and 14). I have, as noted below, used some of his translations and interpretations. The chapter numbers used throughout this section refer to Chin's version.

64. Vol. 3, 10/11a.

65. *Cf.* Irwin's translation, "Soft needle and yielding barb."

66. Vol. 13, 40/9b.

67. Vol. 13, 41/9a.

68. Translation by Irwin.

69. Vol. 1, 3/12b.

70. Irwin, p. 46.

71. Pp. 107–108.

72. Professor Liu Wu-chi in his *An Introduction to Chinese Literature* (Bloomington, 1966), p. 207, praises the artistic achievement

of the novel to the same effect by citing the descriptions of two tiger fights.

73. Lin Yutang, for example, has high praise for Chin both as an individual and as an essayist, and has rendered into English several parts from Chin's commentaries on *Shui-hu* and *Hsi-hsiang*.

74. Quoted in Ch'en Teng-yuan, p. 51.

75. The full text of the episode is in the *Shui-hu Commentary*, vol. 8, 27/13b–19a. Professor Liu Wu-chi in his *An Introduction to Chinese Literature*, pp. 207–208, has translated part of this episode based on the older version. Pearl Buck's translation of the same is found in vol. 1, pp. 382–85. I have consulted both in making my own translation.

76. *I.e.* the ninth time the word "club" has occurred in this chapter, and the third position in which Wu Sung holds his club.

77. *I.e.* Wu Sung, who after hesitating, deliberately chose to confront the tiger. He was not simply forced to meet the tiger. This shows his courage and valor.

78. One of Confucius's disciples, known for his physical strength and impetuosity.

79. 1254–1322. A famous painter of the Yuan period, whose given name was Meng-fu.

80. Chao's wife.

81. As will be seen soon in the following narrative, these are the three things the tiger did in its efforts to seize Wu Sung. What Chin says about Chao Meng-fu's emulation of the horse and Shih Nai-an's complete success in bringing to life Wu Sung's fight with the tiger is of course what we today would call "empathy."

82. Sure sign of the presence of a powerful ghost or spirit.

83. What Chin seems to mean here is that the account is more convincing *because* it departs from literal truth—an indication of Chin's love of paradox.

84. Later as Wu Sung was going down from the ridge, he ran into two hunters disguised as tigers, which created another moment of high suspense in the story. What Chin means here is probably that when Wu Sung's fear (the possibility of another tiger) seemingly comes true later in the story, the surprise felt by the reader is even greater.

85. In *Shu-fang yi-chiao* (*A Corner of My Study*) (Peking, 1944), p. 13.

Chapter Five

1. Arthur Waley, C. C. Wang, and S. I. Hsiung have each made a translation of the story. Waley's version can be found in Cyril Birch (ed.), *Anthology of Chinese Literature* (New York, 1965),

pp. 290–99; Wang's is in his *Traditional Chinese Tales* (New York, 1944), pp. 75–86; and Hsiung's is appended to his *The Romance of the Western Chamber* (New York, reprint 1968), pp. 271–81.

2. Fu Hsi-hua, in his *Hsi-hsiang chi shuo ch'ang chi* (*The Oral and Sung Versions of the Story of Hsi-hsiang chi*) (Shanghai, 1955), has collected a large number of the recitations based on the story of Chang Sheng and Ts'ui Ying-ying.

3. I follow Professor Robert Hightower's translation of the term *chu-kung-tiao*. See *Topics in Chinese Literature* (Cambridge, Mass., 1966, rev. ed.), p. 95.

4. For a detailed account of the development of the story of Ying-ying and Chang Sheng from T'ang to Yuan, see Wang Chi-szu, *Ts'ung Ying-ying chuan tao Hsi-hsiang chi* (*From The Story of Ying-ying to Hsi-hsiang chi*) (Shanghai, 1955). For a searching comparison of the tale, the medley, and the play, see Professor C. T. HSIA's critical introduction to the 1968 reprint of S. I. Hsiung's *The Romance of the Western Chamber*, pp. xiii–xxvi.

5. Cited by TAI PU-FAN in his *Lun Ts'ui Ying-ying*, p. 140.

6. *Kuei Chuang chi* (*Collected Works*) (Shanghai, 1962 ed.), vol. 2, p. 499. For more details on Kuei Chuang's attack on Chin, see below, Chap. 7. Another good example of how the play was treated in a "respectable" "Confucian" family is found in the *Dream of the Red Chamber*. In Chapter 23, we find Pao-yü, the young master and the hero of the novel, in a restless and discontented mood. In an effort to relieve his boredom, one of his intimate servants secured some popular novels and plays for him to read. Pao-yü was greatly pleased. However, being afraid others might find out what he was doing, he selected a safe corner in his room and would only pore over them when no one was around. One day he was caught by Tai-yü, the heroine, in the midst of reading the *Hsi-hsiang chi*. When asked by the latter what he was reading, he could only pretend that it was the *Doctrine of the Mean* and the *Great Learning*, two Confucian classics.

7. *Hsi-hsiang Commentary*, 2/1a (No. 2).

8. *Ibid.*, (No. 1).

9. *Ibid.*, (No. 4). Tr. in consultation w. Ch'en Shou-yi, *op. cit.*, p. 563.

10. *Ibid.*, (No. 3).

11. *Ibid.*

12. *Ibid.*, 7/2a.

13. It is interesting to note that Professor Hightower uses the same argument in defense of the *Chin p'ing mei*. He says, "It is not pornography in that the pornographic element is not the excuse for the

book—though it helps explain the book's popularity." (*Topics in Chinese Literature*, p. 105.)

14. *Hsi-hsiang Commentary*, 2/2a (No. 11). Chin here obviously does not subscribe to the allegorical interpretations of these folk songs, advanced by some other Confucian scholars.

15. See *ibid.*, 2/1a (No. 1).

16. Professor C. T. HSIA in his critical introduction to the reprint of S. I. Hsiung's translation of the play (pp. xxvi–xxix) has also pointed out a few examples of this kind.

17. There are at least twenty-six different editions of the play. By "an older edition of the play," I mean the *Hsi-hsiang chi* published in 1954 by the Tso-chia ch'u-pan-she, under the editorhip of Wu Hsiao-ling. This is a consolidated edition based mainly on the Wang Chi-te edition of the late sixteenth century and the Ling Meng-ch'u edition of early seventeenth century—two editions on which Chin's own edition of the play is believed to have been based. The line quoted below is from p. 5.

18. Translations from the play are mine unless otherwise noted.

19. 4/4b.

20. Reconstruction of these pronunciations is taken from the modern phonetically transcribed edition of Chou Te-ch'ing's (*fl.* 1314) *Chung-yuan yin-yun* (*The Phonology of the Dialect of North China*), known as *Yin-chu Chung-yuan yin-yun* (Taipei, 1962) by Hsü Shih-ying.

21. See *Yin-chu Chung-yuan yin-yun*, pp. 31a and 54b respectively.

22. See Wang Li, *Han-yü shih-lü-hsüeh* (*The Prosody of Chinese Poetry*) (Shanghai, 1964), p. 807, No. 16.

23. P. 80.

24. 6/5a.

25. P. 8.

26. P. 13.

27. 4/9b.

28. 4/8b.

29. *Hsien-ch'ing ou-chi*, p. 65.

30. See note 4, Chapter 4 above, for the translation of *hsieh-tzu* as "Induction."

31. In some Ming editions, therefore, Act II in this part is treated as a *hsieh-tzu*.

32. 2/1a.

33. 4/9b.

34. 7/2b.

35. 7/2b–3a.

36. 7/16a.

37. *Ibid.*

38. 4/3a.

39. *I.e.*, Nos. 15, 16, 17, 25, 26.

40. 2/2b (No. 17).

41. *Ibid.*

42. *Cf.* above, Chap. 2, pp. 22–23.

43. Not counting Part V, which, as we shall soon see, Chin considered a later addition, in the first four parts Chang Sheng and Hung Niang each sing throughout six entire acts, while Ying-ying sings throughout only four entire acts.

44. 2/5a (No. 47).

45. 2/5b (No. 50).

46. 2/5a (No. 48). Note the use of the terminology of the eight-legged essay.

47. 2/5b (No. 49).

48. 4/3a–b.

49. 4/4a.

50. TAI PU-FAN in his *Lun Ts'ui Ying-ying* (pp. 154–86) deals with this point at some length. Although I don't endorse his critical attitude toward Chin, I am nevertheless indebted to him for having called my attention to this aspect of Chin's commentary.

51. P. 7.

52. 4/6b.

53. 4/6a. Note how Chin claims his version of the play to be the authentic one.

54. Pp. 33–34. Parts of this are translated by S. I. Hsiung, *op. cit.*, pp. 44–45.

55. *Cf.* the following section (C), where Chin discusses the "three stages of development" in Ying-ying's love for Chang Sheng.

56. The full text appears in 6/20a–21b. The English translation of the title of each act is taken from S. I. Hsiung, *op. cit.*

57. *I.e.* the first four parts of the paly. As will be shown below in Section D, Chin considered the last part spurious and superfluous, and believed that it should be excised from the play.

58. It is actually the second from the last act, "A Surprising Dream." But Chin felt the play actually could have ended here. See Section D below.

59. Another illustration of Chin's idea of the principle of "indirection" in writing. The personality of one character is revealed through the description of another closely associated with him. Ying-ying and Chang Sheng being what they are, the author cannot but depict Hung Niang in "Love and the Lute" and Ying-ying in "The Fuss about the Billet-doux" the way he does.

60. 5/14a–15a. *Cf.* Chin's idea of "gentleness" and "moderateness"

about literary style toward the end of Section I in Chap. 3 above.

61. 6/13b.

62. See 6/13a–15b, esp. 14b and 15a.

63. In *Yuan Ming Ch'ing hsi-ch'ü yen-chiu lun-wen chi,* pp. 152–170.

64. *Ibid.,* p. 165.

65. *Ibid.,* p. 164, note 1:1.

66. *Ibid.,* p. 166.

67. *Ibid.*

68. Professor C. T. HSIA may be considered an exception. See his critical introduction to S. I. Hsiung's translation of the play, pp. xxii–xxiii.

69. 8/1a.

70. *Yuan Ming Ch'ing hsi-ch'ü yen-chiu lun-wen chi,* p. 165 and note 3.

71. 7/20b. *Cf.* above, Chap. 2, p. 31.

72. See Introductory Remarks to Act IV, Part IV, 7/20a–22a.

73. 8/1b–2a.

74. 8/1b. Again an illustration of Chin's idea of the principle of "indirection."

75. In their joint article, "Chin Sheng-t'an ti wen-hsüeh p'i-p'ing" LIU TA-CHIEH and CHANG P'EI-HENG think Chin does.

76. 8/14b.

77. See above, Chap. 2, beginning of Section II.

78. 2/6a–b (Nos. 61, 62, 63, 64, 67, and 68).

Chapter Six

1. I have counted 187, including four incomplete ones.

2. WILLIAM HUNG, *Tu Fu: China's Greatest Poet* (hereafter, Hung), p. 4.

3. *T'ang Poetry Commentary,* p. 551.

4. See the letter excerpts appended to his *T'ang Poetry Commentary.* Some of his arguments are quite fanciful and whimsical.

5. *Cf.* LIU TA-CHIEH and CHANG P'EI-HENG, "Chin Sheng-t'an ti wen-hsüeh p'i-p'ing" in *Chung-hua wen shih lun-ts'ung,* vol. 3, pp. 161–62.

6. Again note the eight-legged essay terminology here.

7. *Tu Fu Commentary,* 3/27b.

8. *Ibid.,* 1/1b.

9. Translation from Hung, p. 35 (VIII).

10. 1/1a.

11. Both the couplet and Chin's comment appear in 3/8a. Translations from Tu Fu are mine unless otherwise noted.

12. 4/6b. This younger brother was Tu Fu's half-brother, Tu Kuan. See Hung, p. 230.

13. 4/5a–b.

14. 2/29a–b.

15. 2/16b. Translation of the poem taken from Hung, p. 176 (CCII).

16. 2/12b.

17. 2/1b. Translation from Hung, p. 115 (LXXXIX). *Cf.* above, p. 37.

18. See Hung, p. 227.

19. See Hung, p. 227; and YEH CHIA-YING, *Tu Fu Ch'iu-hsing pa-shou chi-shuo* (hereafter, Yeh), pp. 77–78.

20. See Hung, pp. 242–43, 255, 278.

21. See *Tu Fu Commentary*, 3/11a.

22. *Cf.* above, Chapter 3, Section III.

23. This and the following translations from "Autumn Thoughts" are all from A. C. Graham (tr.), *Poems of the Late T'ang* (Baltimore, 1965), pp. 52–55.

24. See Yeh, pp. 99–101.

25. 3/23b; Yeh, p. 102. *"Yu-hsing"* usually means "full of spirits" or "enthusiastic." But, since in the title to these poems the word *"hsing"* clearly suggests random thoughts evoked by the autumn scene, I have thus translated it as "thought-inducing."

26. 3/25a; Yeh, p. 218.

27. 3/24b; Yeh, p. 178.

28. Yeh, p. 178.

29. Also from A. C. Graham, *Poems of the Late T'ang*, p. 20.

30. Pp. 20–22.

31. 3/24a; Yeh, p. 113.

32. Yeh, p. 114.

33. Translation from Hung, p. 116 (LXXXIX).

34. 2/3a.

35. Translation adapted from Hung, p. 125 (XCV).

36. 1/23a.

37. Translation from Hung, p. 51 (XVI).

38. 1/11b.

39. 1/12a.

40. 4/14a. For a full translation of this poem, see Hung, p. 261 (CCCXLVIII).

41. 4/15b. The poem referred to is "Leaving T'an-chou" (Fa T'an-chou).

42. Chin calls them the Twenty Ancient Poems in his commentary because he considers poem 12 in the series to be two poems.

43. See Bibliography (A) for a list of Chin's other commentaries.

Chapter Seven

1. *Ch'u-hsüeh chi* (*A Beginner's Writings*), Szu-pu ts'ung-k'an ed., 43/13a.

2. Preface to the *Ts'ai-tzu pi-tu shu* (*Required Works for Geniuses*). Cited in Ch'en Teng-yuan, pp. 29–30.

3. Pp. 16b–17a.

4. P. 15a.

5. Should be the Sixth.

6. Chin had commented on a few episodes from the *Tso-chuan*, but the book is not one of the *Six Works of Genius*.

7. The four recognized divisions of learning according to the traditional classification.

8. *Kuei Chuang chi* (*Collected Works*) (Shanghai, 1962 ed.), vol. 2, pp. 499–500.

9. *Hsiao-t'ing hsü-lu* (included as a sequel to the *Hsiao-t'ing tsa-lu—Random Jottings in the Hsiao Pavilion*) (Shanghai, n.d.). "Without number to the point of being weird" is a free translation of *"han niu ch'ung tung, niu-kuei she-shen,"* which literally means "[so many as] to make the oxen [bearing them] perspire and to fill [the house] to the rafters (*Mathews'*, 2028:14) and [they are like the] ox-demons and snake-spirits."

10. HU SHIH (Preface to the 120-chapter edition of the *Shui-hu chuan* in *Hu Shih wen-ts'un*, vol. 3, p. 439) and Ch'en Teng-yuan (p. 60) both call this preface a forgery, but neither gives any reason for doing so. CHAO TS'UNG (*Chung-kuo szu ta hsiao-shuo chih yen-chiu*, pp. 118–121) on the one hand seems to think the preface is false, but on the other feels the epithet "The First Work of Genius" was provided by Chin. Perhaps the strongest argument against the authenticity of this preface lies in the fact that as we have seen above in Chapter 3, Section III, Chin himself actually considered the *San-kuo* an artistic failure.

11. *Hu Shih wen-ts'un*, vol. 1, pp. 500–501.

12. *Hu Shih wen-ts'un*, vol. 3, p. 439.

13. "*Shui-hu chuan* k'ao cheng" in *Hu Shih wen-ts'un*, vol. 1, pp. 501–502.

14. Liu's preface is printed in the very beginning of the *Shui-hu Commentary*. His superlative praise of Chin's contribution can be found on pp. 1a, 4b.

15. *The Importance of Living*, p. 130.

16. See above, Chap. 3, Section II D and his short article "T'an Chin Sheng-t'an" in *Lu Hsün ch'üan-chi*, vol. 4, pp. 403–404.

17. *A Brief History of Chinese Fiction*, p. 193.

18. See *Chung-kuo wen-hsüeh shih* (*A History of Chinese Litera-*

ture), compiled by Chung-kuo k'o-hsüeh yuan wen-hsüeh yen-chiu-so Chung-kuo wen-hsüeh shih pien hsieh tsu (Peking, 1962), vol. 3, pp. 855–56.

19. *Ibid.*, p. 741.
20. In *Chung-hua wen shih lun-ts'ung,* vol. 3, pp. 145–62.
21. In *Wen-hsüeh yi-ch'an tseng-k'an,* vol. 9, pp. 12–24.
22. Irwin, p. 94.

Selected Bibliography

(A) A list of Chin's more important commentaries grouped according to genre and arranged approximately in the order in which the works themselves appeared, not in the order in which Chin wrote the commentaries. Since most of the commentaries are collected in the following two works, for the sake of convenience they will be cited in their short forms as follows:

> Collected Works: *Kuan-hua t'ang ts'ai-tzu shu hui-kao* (*Collected Works of Genius of the Kuan-hua Study*). Shanghai: Kuo-kuang shu-chü, 1915 ed., 6 vols.
>
> Required Works: *T'ien-hsia ts'ai-tzu pi-tu shu* (*Required Works for Geniuses of the World*). Shanghai and Peking: Yu-cheng shu-chü, n.d., 6 vols.

(a) Poetry

Book of Poetry (*Collected Works*, vol. 4). Seven poems from the section known as the "Lesser Odes" (Hsiao-ya).

Li Sao (*Collected Works*, vol. 5, in the section called "Sui-shou t'ung" or "Casual Jottings," pp. 6b–10a). Considered by Chin as the *Second Work of Genius* (according to LIAO YEN and the HSIN-CH'OU CHI-WEN, this is the *First Work of Genius*; see Ch'en Teng-yuan, pp. 52–53). Chin, however, only managed to write a foreword and an unfinished preface for it.

Nineteen Ancient Poems (*Collected Works*, vol. 4). Chin calls them Twenty Ancient Poems, poem twelve in the series being divided into two poems.

Tu Fu (712–770) (*Collected Works*, vols. 1–3). *The Fourth Work of Genius*. I have counted altogether 187 poems, several of which have two sets of commentaries.

T'ang ts'ai-tzu shih [*chia-chi*] ([*A First Collection of*] *Poems by Geniuses of T'ang*). Taipei: Te-chih ch'u-pan-she, 1963 ed. Some 595 Regulated Verse poems of the seven-syllable type by 145 poets.

Ou-yang Hsiu (1007–1072) (*Collected Works*, vol. 5). 12 *tz'u* poems.

147

(b) Prose

Tso-chuan, or *Tso Commentary* (*Required Works*, vol. 1, *chüan* 1–2, and vol. 6, addenda; *Collected Works*, vol. 4). *Required Works* contains forty-eight episodes, and *Collected Works* five. Two of these episodes, however, appear in both collections (though commentaries for them differ), thus reducing the total number of episodes to fifty-one.

Kuo-yü, or *Conversations from the States* (*Required Works*, vol. 1, *chüan* 3). Twenty-eight episodes.

Mencius (*Collected Works*, vol. 4). The first four sections of Chapter 1.

Chuang-tzu (*Collected Works*, vol. 5, "Sui-shou t'ung," pp. 1a–2a). Considered by Chin as the *First Work of Genius* (according to LIAO YEN and the *HSIN-CH'OU CHI-WEN*, this is the *Second Work of Genius*; see Ch'en Teng-yuan, pp. 52–53). Again Chin wrote only two brief notes on the meaning of "Nan-hua [ching]," another title for the works of Chuang-tzu.

Chan-kuo ts'e, or *Intrigues of the Warring States* (*Required Works*, vol. 2, *chüan* 4–5). Thirty-seven episodes.

Shih-chi (*Required Works*, vols. 3–4, *chüan* 7–8; and vol. 6, addenda). The *Third Work of Genius*. Includes eighty-five "appraisals" (*tsan, i.e.* personal comments by Szu-ma Ch'ien usually placed at the end of a chapter), two prefaces, and one biography (of Po-yi). Included are also some items without commentary.

Han Yü (768–824) (*Required Works*, vols. 4–5, *chüan* 10–11). Thirty pieces.

Liu Tsung-yuan (773–819) (*Required Works*, vol. 5, *chüan* 12). Seventeen pieces.

Ou-yang Hsiu (1007–1072). (*Required Works*, vol. 5, *chüan* 13). Eighteen pieces.

Su Shih (*Su Tung-p'o*, 1037–1101). (*Required Works*, vol. 6, *chüan* 14). Nineteen pieces.

(c) Vernacular Literature

Kuan-hua t'ang yuan-pen Shui-hu chuan: Ti-wu ts'ai-tzu shu (*Kuan-hua Study's Orginal Edition of the Shui-hu chuan: The Fifth Work of Genius*). Shanghai: Chung-hua Book Co., 1934 (a photolithographic reproduction), 24 vols.

Hui-t'u Hsi-hsiang chi: Ti-liu ts'ai-tzu shu (*Illustrated Hsi-hsiang chi: The Sixth Work of Genius*). Shanghai: Sao-yeh shan-fang, 1918 ed., 4 vols.

(B) Secondary Sources (confined to those most useful for the present study).

ABRAMS, M. H. *The Mirror and the Lamp.* New York: Oxford University Press, 1953. A classic study of the esthetics and literary criticism of the Romantic period. I have found it most useful in my effort to categorize Chin Sheng-t'an's general theory on literature.

CHANG, YU-LUAN. "Chin Sheng-t'an tsen-yang wu-mieh Sung Chiang ti" (How Chin Sheng-t'an slandered Sung Chiang), in *Shui-hu yen-chiu lun-wen chi (Critical Essays on Shui-hu)*. Peking: Tso-chia ch'u-pan-she, 1957, pp. 324–31. A good study marred by the author's obvious prejudices against Chin.

CHAO, TS'UNG. *Chung-kuo szu ta hsiao-shuo chih yen-chiu (Studies in Four Major Chinese Novels)*. Hong Kong: Yu-lien ch'u-pan-she, 1964. A collection of four substantial essays originally intended as prefaces to the four traditional novels he recently edited: *Shui-hu chuan, San-kuo yen-yi (Romance of the Three Kingdoms), Hsi-yu chi (Pilgrimage to the West, or Monkey)*, and *Hung-lou meng (Dream of the Red Chamber)*.

CH'EN, TENG-YUAN. *Chin Sheng-t'an chuan (A Biography of Chin Sheng-t'an)*. Shanghai: The Commercial Press, 1935. The most comprehensive biography of Chin in Chinese. Highly informative, but lacks focus and organization.

CHOU, TSO-JEN. *Chung-kuo hsin-wen-hsüeh ti yuan-liu (The Origins of China's New Literature)*. Peking: Jen-wen shu-tien, 1934 (revised ed.). Traces the origins of China's new literature all the way back to the Kung-an School of the 16th century.

——. "T'an Chin Sheng-t'an" ("About Chin Sheng-t'an"), *Jen-chien shih*, No. 31 (July 5, 1935), pp. 3–5. Also in his *K'u-chu tsa-chi (Miscellaneous Jottings of Bitter Bamboo)*. Shanghai: Liang-yu fu-hsing t'u-shu yin-shua kung-szu, 1940, pp. 10–20. A highly informative essay, especially about the more eccentric aspects of Chin's life, written in a charming informal style.

CHU, CHAO-NIEN. "Tsen-yang p'ing-chia Chin Jen-jui ti wen-hsüeh li-lun—chien t'an Chin-p'i *Hsi-hsiang chi*" ("How to Evaluate the Literary Theory of Chin Jen-jui: an Examination of His Commentary on the *Hsi-hsiang chi*"), in *Wen-hsüeh yi-ch'an tseng-k'an (A Supplement to the Literary Heritage Series)*. Peking: Chung-hua Book Co., 1962, vol. 9, pp. 12–24. Represents the most objective reassessment of Chin Sheng-t'an by a Marxist critic.

FANG, CHAO-YING. "Chin Jen-jui", in Arthur W. Hummel (ed.). *Eminent Chinese of the Ch'ing Period*. Washington, D.C.: U.S. Government Printing Office, 1943/1944, vol. 1, pp. 164–65. A judicious study of Chin's life, although the attribution of his motives for undertaking to comment on the *Shui-hu chuan* and *Hsi-hsiang chi* is somewhat misleading.

Ho, Hsin. *Shui-hu yen-chiu* (*Studies in Shui-hu*). Shanghai: Ku-tien wen-hsüeh ch'u-pan-she, 1957 (new ed.). A good, solid textual study on the subject.

Ho, Man-tzu. *Lun Chin Sheng-t'an p'ing kai Shui-hu chuan* (*On Chin Sheng-t'an's Critique and Revision of the Shui-hu chuan*). Shanghai: Shanghai ch'u-pan kung-szu, 1954. A typical example of the Communist effort to vilify Chin.

Hsia, C. T. *The Classic Chinese Novel*. New York: Columbia University Press, 1968. A reevaluation of six major Chinese novels largely from a Western point of view. Exciting, stimulating, and thought-provoking. The best there is in the field.

————. "A Critical Introduction" to *The Romance of the Western Chamber*, translated by S. I. Hsiung. New York: Columbia University Press, 1968 (a reprint), pp. xi–xxxii. An exciting re-reading of the play.

Hsin-ch'ou chi-wen (*A Chronicle of the Year Hsin-ch'ou, i.e.* 1661), in *Shen-pao kuan ts'ung-shu hsü-chi* (*A Supplement to the Collected Works Series of the Shen-pao kuan*), Part 4 (Columbia University Library microfilm). A first-hand account of the circumstances of Chin's death, with a short general biography of him.

Hu, Shih. "Shui-hu chuan k'ao-cheng" ("A Textual Study of the *Shui-hu chuan*"), in his *Hu Shih wen-ts'un* (*Collected Works of Hu Shih*). Taipei: Yuan-tung t'u-shu kung-szu, 1953, vol. 1, pp. 500–47. Though outdated, it still has value as one of the very first major "scientific" investigations of the novel: the evolution of its text and its authorship.

————. "Pai-erh-shih hui pen chung-yi *Shui-hu chuan* hsü" ("Preface to the 120-Chapter Edition of the *Shui-hu chuan*"), in *Hu Shih wen-ts'un*, vol. 3, pp. 404–42. A further investigation of the novel based on new information.

Hung, William. *Tu Fu: China's Greatest Poet*. Cambridge (Mass.): Harvard University Press, 1952. The best biographical study of Tu Fu in English, with a generous amount of translations from the poet's works.

Huo, Sung-lin. "Chin Sheng-t'an p'i kai *Hsi-hsiang chi* ti fan-tung yi-t'u" ("Chin Sheng-t'an's Reactionary Intentions in His Critique and Revision of the *Hsi-hsiang chi*"), in *Wen-hsüeh yi-ch'an hsüan-chi* (*Selected Essays from Literary Heritage*). Peking: Tso-chia ch'u-pan-she, 1956, vol. 1, pp. 218–27. Another example of the Communist attack on Chin.

Irwin, Richard G. *The Evolution of a Chinese Novel: Shui Hu Chuan*. Cambridge (Mass.): Harvard University Press, 1953. A solid study on the subject. Some of the conclusions here have since been revised in his "Water Margin Revisited," *T'oung Pao,* XLVIII: 4–5 (1960), pp. 393–415. Contains a few bibliographical items on Chin Sheng-t'an.

KARASHIMA, TAKESHI. "Kin Sei-tan no shōgai to sono bungei hihyo" ("The Life and Literary Criticism of Chin Sheng-t'an"), in *Chosen Shina bunka no kenkyu* (*Studies in the Culture of Korea and China*), edited by Keijō teikoku daigaku Hobungakukai, 1929, pp. 537–603. The most extensive study of Chin Sheng-t'an I have seen in Japanese.

———. "Kin Sei-tan" ("Chin Sheng-t'an"), in *Chūgoku no shisōka* (*China's Thinkers*), compiled by the Chūgoku tetsugaku kenkyu-shitsu of Tokyo University. Tokyo: Keisō shobō, 1963, vol. 2, pp. 642–53. Just a shorter version of his former study, with no new information.

K'u-miao chi-lüeh (*A Brief Record of the Incident of Lamenting in the Temple*), the second item in *T'ung-shih* (*Bitter History*). Shanghai: The Commercial Press, 1912 (4th ed.). Another first-hand account of the circumstances relating to Chin's death.

KUO, SHAO-YÜ. *Chung-kuo wen-hsüeh p'i-p'ing shih* (*A History of Chinese Literary Criticism*). Shanghai: The Commercial Press, 1947, 2 vols. The most comprehensive treatment of the subject by a noted scholar who has devoted most of his life to the study of Chinese literary criticism. Regrettably, however, Chin's criticism is completely overlooked in the book.

LÉVY, ANDRÉ. "Un Document sur la Querelle des Anciens et des Modernes More Sinico," *T'oung Pao,* LIV: 4–5 (1968), pp. 251–274. Primarily a translation of Yuan Tsung-tao's essay "On Writing," it gives a succinct summary of the quarrels between the Antiquarians and the Kung-an School.

LI, YÜ. *Hsien-ch'ing ou-chi* (*Occasional Jottings in Leisure Time*). Shanghai: Pei-yeh shan-fang, 1936. Contains the most fair-minded and judicious evaluation of Chin's commentary on the *Hsi-hsiang chi.*

LIAO, YEN. "Chin Sheng-t'an Hsien-sheng chuan" ("A Biography of Mr. Chin Sheng-t'an"), in his *Erh-shih-ch'i sung-t'ang chi* (*Collected Works of the Hall of Twenty-seven Pines*), a reprint by the Commercial Press and Pao-yuan yin-wu-chü of Shao-chou (prefaces dated 1928), 6/5a–6a. A short sympathetic account of Chin's life.

LIN, YUTANG. *The Importance of Living.* New York: The John Day Co., 1937 (39th impression). Contains translations of the thirty-three delights in life (pp. 131–36) and the art of travel (pp. 334–38), both from Chin's commentary on the *Hsi-hsiang chi.*

———. *The Importance of Understanding* (Translations from the

Chinese). Cleveland: The World Publishing Co., 1960. Contains translations of Chin's two prefaces to the *Hsi-hsiang chi* (pp. 75–82), and his forged preface to the *Shui-hu chuan* (pp. 83–85).

LIU, JAMES J. Y. *The Art of Chinese Poetry.* Chicago: The University of Chicago Press, 1962. The best study on the subject in any language.

LIU, TA-CHIEH AND CHANG, P'EI-HENG. "Chin Sheng-t'an ti wen-hsüeh p'i-p'ing" ("The Literary Criticism of Chin Sheng-t'an"), in *Chung-hua wen shih lun-ts'ung* (*Collected Essays on Chinese Literature and History*). Peking: Chung-hua Book Co., 1963, vol. 3, pp. 145–62. The best and most objective reevaluation of Chin's criticism that has come out of the Chinese mainland to date.

[LIU, TA-CHIEH.] *Chung-kuo wen-hsüeh fa-ta shih* (*A History of the Flourishing of Chinese Literature*). Taipei: Taiwan Chung-hua Book Co., 1967. Still one of the best and most comprehensive histories of Chinese literature.

LU HSÜN. *A Brief History of Chinese Fiction,* translated by Yang Hsien-yi and Gladys Yang. Peking: Foreign Language Press, 1964 (2nd ed.). This is the English version of his *Chung-kuo hsiao-shuo shih-lüeh* (revised 1930). Still sound and useful.

———. "T'an Chin Sheng-t'an" ("About Chin Sheng-t'an"), in *Lu Hsün ch'üan-chi* (*Complete Works of Lu Hsün*). Peking: Jen-min wen-hsüeh ch'u-pan-she, 1957, vol. 4, pp. 403–404. A derogatory and unfair appraisal of Chin.

TAI, PU-FAN. *Lun Ts'ui Ying-ying* (*On Ts'ui Ying-ying*). Shanghai: Shanghai wen-yi ch'u-pan-she, 1963. Contains a discussion of Chin's revisions of the *Hsi-hsiang chi* as they relate to the character of Ying-ying.

WANG, CHI-SZU. "Hsi-hsiang chi hsü shuo" ("Notes on the *Hsi-hsiang chi*"), in *Yuan Ming Ch'ing hsi-ch'ü yen-chiu lun-wen chi* (*Studies in the Drama of Yuan, Ming, and Ch'ing—a Collection of Essays*), edited by Tso-chia ch'u-pan-she pien-chi-pu. Peking: Tso-chia ch'u-pan-she, 1957, pp. 152–70. A good, scholarly piece.

YANG, KUNG-TAO. *Chin Sheng-t'an yi-shih* (*Anecdotes about Chin sheng-t'an*). Nanking(?): Liang-yu hsien, 1921 (2nd ed.). A handy piece for those interested in the topic.

YEH, CHIA-YING (Mrs. Chao). *Tu Fu Ch'iu-hsing pa-shou chi-shuo* (*A Critical Anthology of Commentaries on Tu Fu's "Autumn Thoughts," Eight Poems*). Taipei: Chung-hua ts'ung-shu pien-shen wei-yuan hui, 1966. A collection of comments on the eight poems by some thirty-five traditional commentators, accompanied by sound and perceptive remarks from Professor Yeh herself.

Index

The listing of book and article titles in the index is not meant to be exhaustive. Those already listed in Bibliography (B), for example, are generally not included here.

153